THE CITIZENS LAW LIBRARY

Harper Hamilton's
LAW FOR THE LAYMAN SERIES

HOW TO
BE YOUR OWN
LAWYER
IN COURT

"In all courts of the United States the parties may plead and conduct their own cases personally or by counsel as, by the rules of such courts, respectively, are permitted to manage and conduct causes therein." 28 U.S.C. 1654

YOUR LEGAL RIGHT TO REPRESENT
YOURSELF IN COURT
COURT RULES
STATE AND FEDERAL COURTS
COMPLAINTS
ANSWERS
PLEADINGS
DEPOSITIONS
NOTICES
DISCOVERY
TRIAL PREPARATION
STRATEGY TO END LITIGATION
WITHOUT TRIAL
TRIAL TECHNIQUES & STRATEGY
POST TRIAL MANEUVERS
SMALL CLAIMS COURTS
FORMS
GLOSSARY OF TERMS

By HARPER HAMILTON

HAMILTON PRESS

TABLE OF CONTENTS

Preface

The judicial system in this country has been under intensive study and "reform" since 1904! The lawyers, judges, politicians and law professors just talk--talk--talk; they organize committees and write impressive "Reports." But the court system has simply broken down and there appears to be little chance of improvement even though the Chief Justice of the United States has been yelling and screaming at lawyers for years to get their act together.

Many lawyers charge $100 to $400 or more per hour for their legal services. And all lawyers have "short hours" and "long hours" in setting their fees--meaning they charge all the traffic will bear! Cases drag on and on and on ad infinitum--and legal fees just keep rolling on and on. And the bad part is that the modern trial is more a gladiator's duel in which the lawyers have one eye on the grand stands--the other eye on their own pocketbook, and somehow the interests of the client--the American litigant--gets altogether lost in the "fascination with procedures." Lost With The Winds!

The end result is that one of society's most "noble" professions--the legal profession--has utterly failed in its foremost obligations to society; lawyers have not only failed to take any definitive measures to improve--or "reform"--the system--they stand around-- in a lackadaisical stupor--and watch the courts become more overcrowded, less efficient, filled with politi- cal appointments, and essentially in a state of severe inability to adequately meet the needs of the general public.

Now, what to do? Well, let's join them. Yes, You Can Be Your Own Lawyer In Court. If it takes a typical case one--two--three or more years to wind its way through the court system and costs both liti- gants a fortune--why can't you simply learn these cute little "procedures" the lawyers are so "fasci- nated" with and bring your case to a close all by yourself and save all those legal fees. If you learn all the "techniques" and "strategies" the lawyers use routinely to drag out and complicate cases, you can (1) have a lot of fun, (2) save a bundle of money in legal fees and expenses, (3) save money on the case by settling on your own terms, (4) save it all by winning the case, (5) do a better job than a lawyer, and (6) generally have a blast by kicking up a lot of dust just for the heck of it!

But, let's get one thing straight: when you get

to court, let's have no more of the "nice guy" business.
When a dispute gets to court its time to roll up your
sleeves, put on the iron knuckles and stand up tall
and fight! Don't make the mistake of believing your
adversary in court will ever be a friend of yours.
No. I guarantee you: He will kick you in at every
turn--and his lawyer is capable of, and probably will,
cut your throat at the drop of a hat. Second, you
must play the "game" strictly in accordance with the
rules and the law. That's what this book is all about.
Keep your cool. Third, be ethical, honest, but tough.

With the proper use of discovery "techniques,"
and trial "tactics" you can be in command all the way.
Carefully schedule your pleadings, discovery, hearings,
and procedures to conform with your interests and
desires--and convenience. You can be in control all
the way.

What about pro se (in person; in his own behalf;
do it yourself) litigation rather than paying a "pro-
fessional" to handle your case? Voltaire once said:

Only twice in my life have I felt utterly ruined:
once when I lost a lawsuit and once when I won.

Little does it matter that you "win" a $1000 law-
suit if it costs you $2000 in lawyer fees.

A recent law review article suggests:

Too often, the bar and the bench have regarded,
treated, and disposed of those who proceed without counsel as, at best, outsiders. As a result
all parties lose--not only the pro se petitioner,
but also those who presume that the pro se
petitioner has a worthless claim, or worse,
that he himself is somehow worthless because
he has no counsel. There are those who recognize that the opportunity to proceed without
counsel in our system prevents a strangle-hold
on justice by lawyers. (Emphasis added) Pro
Se Litigation: The Misunderstood Pro Se Litigant: More Than A Pawn In The Game by John
P. Flannery and Ira P. Robbins, 41 Brooklyn
Law Review 769, Spring 1975.

The libraries are filled with books that pro-
nounce the greatness of our American way of life--
including our judicial system--and there are an equal
number of books that blast the court system as "rotten
to the roots."

This book doesn't take off on any of those trails;
we tell you how to come out a winner when you go to
court. That's what this book is about.

CHAPTER I

YOUR RIGHT TO DEFEND YOURSELF IN COURT

You have a legal right to represent yourself--
be your own lawyer--in court. Our society has recently
experienced some unusual traumas with lawyers--judges--
courts--politicians and unethical scoundrels. Although
lawyers may not be the "sole" cause of these phenomena,
they sure led the parade! Our laws (thousands of them)
and our courts (thousands of them) don't seem to be
able to keep the barn door shut; and when it swings
open--out comes a Watergate or Koreagate. All the
Kings Men can't put them back in the barn.

Mistrust of lawyers, courts and judges was one
of the major considerations that motivated the Found-
ing Fathers to write the Federal Constitution as they
did. The U.S. Supreme Court recently said:

> In the American Colonies the insistence upon a
> right of self-representation was, if anything,
> more fervent than in England.
>
> The colonists brought with them an appreciation
> of self-reliance and a traditional distrust of
> lawyers. When the Colonies were first settled,
> "the lawyer was synonymous with the cringing
> Attorneys-General and Solicitors-General of the
> Crown and the arbitrary Justices of the King's
> Court, all bent on the conviction of those who
> opposed the King's prerogatives, and twisting
> the law to secure convictions." This prejudice
> gained strength in the Colonies where "distrust

of lawyers became an institution." Several Colonies prohibited pleading for hire in the 17th century. The prejudice persisted into the 18th century as "the lower classes came to identify lawyers with the upper class." The years of Revolution and Confederation saw an upsurge of antilawyer sentiment, a "sudden revival, after the War of the Revolution, of the old dislike and distrust of lawyers as a class." In the heat of these sentiments the Constitution was forged.

This is not to say that the Colonies were slow to recognize the value of counsel in criminal cases. Colonial judges soon departed from ancient English practice and allowed accused felons the aid of counsel for their defense. At the same time, however, the basic right of self-representation was never questioned. We have found no instance where a colonial court required a defendant in a criminal case to accept as his representative an unwanted lawyer. Indeed, even where counsel was permitted, the general practice continued to be self-representation.

Faretta v. California, 422 U.S. 806 (1975)

On May 27, 1977, Chief Justice Burger, at an American Bar Association Conference told the lawyers what he thought about the "legal profession." A newspaper article, May 28, 1977, told the story as follows:

> Chief Justice Warren E. Burger warned Friday that unless more legal disputes are settled outside the courtroom the United States could be "over-run by hordes of lawyers hungry as locusts."
>
> Burger, an advocate of court reform, turned his attention to the legal profession in a speech to the American Bar Association, contending that lawyers, judges and law professors had developed

a "fascination with procedure" that may have led ". . . to a smug assumption that conflicts can be solved only by law-trained people."

Non-lawyer, he suggested, could help settle many disputes cheaper and faster.

The harsh truth is that unless we devise substitutes for the courtroom processes, we may be on our way to a society overrun by hordes of lawyers hungry as locusts and brigades of judges in numbers never before contemplated, he said.

The Chief Justice's remarks were made in a speech at an ABA conference in New York on new ways to settle "minor" legal disputes--such as small claims, landlord-tenant conflicts and consumer complaints. A copy of the text was made available in Washington.

An assembly sponsored by the American Bar Association recently reported about the American probate system that:

The bar should encourage the trend toward various devices permitting settlement of estates with little or no court involvement (in the absence of controversy) and with only minimally necessary involvement of lawyers. The development of procedures for transferring property without administration should be encouraged, as should "do-it-yourself techniques."

American Bar Association Journal, January 1977, Page 88.

During the past few years our court system has continued to deteriorate--rather than improve--and it is more overcrowded now than ever before--and cases are clogging the court calendars--and the legal system

simply can't seem to cope with the proliferation
of litigation. See, for example, a telling story on
the current court situation in "The Chilling Impact
of Litigation, Easier Access to the Courts Means
Skyrocketing Costs and Interminable Delays," Legal
Affairs, Business Week, June 6, 1977, Page 58.

In response to this unmanageable situation there
has recently been made available to the general public
a wide variety of do-it-yourself legal guides covering
such subjects as estate planning, forming your own
corporation, writing your own will, landlord-tenant
disputes, no fault divorce guides and many others.
In fact, this book is one in a series of legal guides
for laymen comprising The Citizens Law Library.

This book has been planned, designed, written and
published to help you handle your own case in court
without a lawyer and without staggering legal fees
and expenses, and to avoid getting overrun "by the
hordes."

With respect to your legal right to represent
yourself in court without a lawyer, the United States
Supreme Court, in the Faretta Case, said:

> In the federal courts, the right of self-repre-
> sentation has been protected by statute since
> the beginnings of our Nation. Section 35 of
> the Judiciary Act of 1789, 1 Stat. 73, 92,

enacted by the First Congress and signed by
President Washington one day before the Sixth
Amendment was proposed, provided that 'in all
the courts of the United States, the parties may
plead and manage their own causes personally or
by the assistance of . . . counsel . . .'
The right is currently codified in 28 U.S.C.
Sec 1654.

With few exceptions, each of the several States
also accords a defenaant the right to represent
himself in any criminal case. The Constitutions
of 36 States explicitly confer that right.
Moreover, many state courts have expressed the
view that the right is also supported by the
Constitution of the United States.

Faretta v. California, 422 U.S. 806 (1975)

In Adams v. United States ex rel. McCann, 317

U.S. 260, 279, the Supreme Court said:

The right to assistance of counsel and the
correlative right to dispense with a lawyer's
help are not legal formalisms. They rest on
considerations that go to be substance of an
accused's position before the law . . .

What were contrived as protections for the
accused should not be turned into fetters . . .
To deny an accused a choice of procedure in
circumstances in which he, though a layman, is
as capable as any lawyer of making an intelli-
gent choice, is to impair the worth of great
Constitutional safeguards by treating them as
empty verbalisms.

When the administration of the criminal law . . .
is hedged about as it is by the Constitutional
safeguards for the protection of an accused, to
deny him in the exercise of his free choice the
right to dispense with some of these safeguards
. . . is to imprison a man in his privileges and
call it the Constitution.

The Faretta case, which settled the issue in criminal cases, was summed up by the court's opinion as follows:

> The Sixth and Fourteenth Amendments of our Constitution guarantee that a person brought to trial in any state or federal court must be afforded the right to the assistance of counsel before he can be validly convicted and punished by imprisonment. This clear constitutional rule has emerged from a series of cases decided here over the last 50 years. The question before us now is whether a defendant in a state criminal trial has a constitutional right to proceed without counsel when he voluntarily and intelligently elects to do so. Stated another way, the question is whether a State may constitutionally hale a person into its criminal courts and there force a lawyer upon him, even when he insists that he wants to conduct his own defense. It is not an easy question, but we have concluded that a State may not constitutionally do so.

> Faretta v. California, 422 U.S. 806 (1975)

Although the Faretta case related specifically to criminal cases, the principle would apply with equal force to civil cases. In an annotation in 67 American Law Reports, Second 1103, it is said:

> The cases herein are in substantial agreement with the general proposition that a party in a civil action may appear either pro se or through counsel (pursuant to statute in some instances), but that he has no absolute right to do both in the absence of express statutory or constitutional provision.

> The Georgia Constitution, Article 1, Section 1,

provides:

No person shall be deprived of the right to
prosecute or defend his own cause in any of the
courts of this State, in person, by attorney,
or both.

Most other states have a similar provision
either in the constitution or by statute.

The mere fact that you have a legal right to
represent yourself in court does not necessarily
mean that you should always dispense with the services of a lawyer. Fact is, we think there are some
well defined cases in which you must have a lawyer's
help to get the protection you need; and there are
well defined cases (described herein) where you
might be better off without a lawyer. You be the
judge!

In the Faretta case one of the three dissenting
judges said:

> If there is any truth to the old proverb that
> 'one who is his own lawyer has a fool for a
> client,' the court by its opinion today now
> bestows a constitutional right on one to
> make a fool of himself.

Another judge said:

> Pro se representation may at times serve the
> ideal of a fair trial better than representation
> by an attorney.

U.S. ex rel Soto v. U.S. (3rd Cir Pa) 504 F 2d
1339

The "Standards Relating to Trial Courts" prepared
by the American Bar Association Commission on Stanards
of Judicial Administration, approved by the American
Bar Association House of Delegates in February, 1976
provides as follows:

> 2.23 Conduct of Cases Where Litigants Appear
> Without Counsel. When a litigant undertakes
> to represent himself, the court should take
> whatever measures may be reasonable and nec-
> essary to insure a fair trial.
>
> Commentary
>
> The duty of the courts to make their procedures
> fair is not limited to appointing counsel for
> eligible persons who request representation.
> In many instances, persons who cannot afford
> counsel are ineligible for appointed counsel;
> in other cases, persons who can afford counsel,
> or who are eligible to be provided with counsel,
> refuse to be represented. The refusal may be
> grounded on the litigant's belief that if he
> has counsel he will be denied any opportunity
> to speak for himself, that only through personal
> presentation of his case can he really make known
> the merits of his case, that no lawyer will faith-
> fully represent him at a fair fee, or that the
> judicial system is so inherently unjust that his
> only chance for a fair trial is to represent him-
> self. In other instances, the litigant may
> believe, reasonably or unreasonably, that the
> matter in controversy is one in which it is not
> worth retaining counsel, even though his case
> is genuinely meritorious and even though the
> opposing party may have found it in his own
> interest to retain counsel. In criminal cases,
> an accused has, at least under some circumstances,
> a federally guaranteed right to represent himself.
> Faretta v. California, 422 U.S. 806 (1975).
>
> All such situations present great difficulties
> for the court because the court's essential role
> as an impartial arbiter cannot be performed with

the usual confidence that the merits of the case will be fully disclosed through the litigant's presentations. These difficulties are compounded when, as can often be the case, the litigant's capability even as a lay participant appears limited by gross ignorance, inarticulateness, naivete, or mental disorder. They are especially great when one party is represented by counsel and the other is not, for intervention by the court introduces not only ambiguity and potential conflict in the court's role but also consequent ambiguity in the role of counsel for the party who is represented. Yet it is ultimately the judge's responsibility to see that the merits of a controversy are resolved fairly and justly. Fulfilling that responsibility may require that the court, while remaining neutral in consideration of the merits, assume more than a merely passive role in assuring that the merits are adequately presented.

The proper scope of the court's responsibility is necessarily an expression of careful exercise of judicial discretion and cannot be fully described by specific formula. Legal corollaries of the right to counsel and the experience of conscientious judges establish certain guidelines. Where a litigant is entitled to be provided with assistance of counsel, but indicates a desire to represent himself, the court should fully advise him of his right to representation and the importance of availing himself of it. The court should strongly discourage waiver of counsel by a litigant entitled to the appointment of counsel and should require the litigant to consult with a lawyer before accepting a waiver of the right. American Bar Association Standards, The Function of the Trial Judge Sec. 6.6; Providing Defense Services Sec. 7.31. Where the litigant appears primarily interested in an opportunity to state his case personally to the court or jury, he should be assured that he will have reasonable opportunity to speak for himself and may thereby be persuaded to accept the assistance of counsel. In some circumstances it may be appropriate to appoint standby counsel. American Bar Association Standards, The Function of the Trial Judge Sec. 6.7.

Where a litigant has no right to be provided
with counsel, the court in appropriate cases
should urge him to retain counsel and facilitate
an appropriate referral to the bar for that
purpose. Where a litigant represents himself,
the court in the interest of fair determination
of the merits should ask such questions and sug-
gest the production of such evidence as may be
necessary to supplement or clarify the litigant's
presentation of the case.

In the final analysis you will have to review

the guidelines set out in this book, study your own

case carefully and make your own decision based on

your particular situation. Don't hesitate to ask a

lawyer his opinion on this question. Once you decide

to represent yourself--tear 'em up Tiger!

One final admonition: don't get the idea that

your legal right to handle your own case in court is

absolute--or gets you home free. You must obey all

court rules--and the judge has an almost unlimited

discretion in "throwing" you out of court if you

don't know how to proceed in an orderly procedure.

Follow the instructions given in this book--and

you'll make it!

CHAPTER II

HOW THE TRIAL COURT SYSTEM WORKS

A. The Federal Courts

The federal system consists of the following:

1. United States Supreme Court.

2. U.S. Courts of Appeals (11).

3. U.S. District Courts (at least one in each state).

4. Other courts which we are not here concerned with, including U.S. Court of Customs and Patent Appeals, U.S. Court of Claims, Tax Court of the United States, U.S. Customs Court, and U.S. Court of Military Appeals.

The federal courts have jurisdiction in the following:

1. Cases in law and equity arising under the U.S. Constitution, the laws of the United States and treaties--called "federal question jurisdiction." 28 U.S.C. 1331.

2. Cases affecting ambassadors, counsels, etc.

3. Cases of admiralty and maritime jurisdiction.

4. Cases to which the U.S. is a party.

5. Controversies between two or more states, or between a state and a citizen of another state.

6. Controversies between citizens of different states--

diversity jurisdiction--or between citizens and foreign nationals. 28 U.S.C. 1332.

B. State Courts

The state court systems vary greatly in the patterns, names, and organization of courts, however they fall into the following broad groups:

1. State Court of Last Resort generally called Supreme Court, Court of Appeals, Supreme Judicial Court, Supreme Court of Errors, and other similar names.

2. Intermediate Appellate Courts called by various names.

3. Trial Courts of General Jurisdiction

4. Trial Courts of Limited or Special Jurisdiction.

5. Local Trial Courts sometimes called Traffic Court, Police Court, Small Claims Court, Justice of the Peace Court, Alderman's Court, Magistrate Court, Town Court, Parish Court, Mayor's Court, etc.

The "subject matter" of state courts vary from state to state, but the general pattern is to have:

1. A trial court of general jurisdiction usually called Superior Court, District Court, Circuit Court, and other names. This is the main trial court in the state.

2. Courts of "limited" or "special" jurisdiction-- usually a civil court that handles cases involving amounts up to specified amounts--typically $5,000 to

$10,000. Special probate courts, juvenile courts, domestic relations courts, small claims courts, Justice Courts, Magistrates Court, and Mayor's Court are examples of other names given to these courts.

By way of example the trial courts of California are as follows:

1. Superior Court (general jurisdiction): There is one Superior Court in every county of the state, but there are branches in more populous counties. The Superior Court has subject matter jurisdiction as follows:

a. Over all civil litigation in actions at law where the amount demanded (exclusive of interest) or the value of the property in controversy is in excess of $5,000. (One exception: If the county has no municipal court, then the Superior Court's jurisdictional minimum is $500.)

b. General equity jurisdiction, regardless of the amount involved (injunctions, declaratory relief, specific performance, etc).

c. Exclusive jurisdiction over probate, divorce; and actions involving title to real property or the legality of a tax. California Constitution, Article IV, Section 5, 6.

2. Municipal Court (limited jurisdiction): One in
each judicial district created by the state, having
a population of 40,000 or more. If less than the
requisite population, there is no municipal court.
This court has subject matter jurisdiction as follows:

   a. Over all actions at law where the amount
demanded (exclusive of interest) or the value of the
property in controversy is $5,000 or less.

   b. In certain equitable actions, for example,
to quiet title to personal property valued at $5,000
or less; partnership dissolutions where the assets
are $5,000 or less; rescission of contracts if in-
cidental to a claim of $5,000 or less; foreclosure of
certain liens where the total claim is $5,000 or less,
and the total claim is $5,000 or less.

   c. Provided the action is within its original
jurisdiction a municipal court may consider any equitable defense, for example, laches, estoppel, etc; may
grant temporary restraining orders and injunctions
(equitable relief); and may impose liability whether
the theory upon which liability is sought to be imposed
involves legal or equitable principles.

3. Justice Court: (limited jurisdiction): At least
one in every county of the state and one in every

judicial district having a population of less than 40,000. A Justice Court has subject matter jurisdiction as follows:

    a. Over all actions at law where amount demanded (exclusive of interest) is $1,000 or less.

    b. Very limited equitable jurisdiction, for example, to foreclose liens on personal property when the lien is $1,000 or less; of unlawful detainer actions where the rental value is $300 or less per month. California Constitution, Article VI, Sections 1, 5, 6, 11. CCP 89, 112.

    C. Jurisdiction

    Essentially the term jurisdiction means two things: (1) is this the right court to determine this issue (subject matter jurisdiction), and (2) does the court have the legal power over the parties (in personam jurisdiction).

1. In Personam (personal) Jurisdiction

    Where a plaintiff seeks to impose liability upon a defendant, as opposed merely to determining rights of property, or to obtain an order binding the defendant personally, in personam jurisdiction is required.

    To subject a person to the jurisdiction of a court there must be proper service of process. This may be done by personal service or by constructive

service or substituted service. In all events there
is a constitutional requirement of sufficient contact
with a jurisdiction to warrant the exercise of jurisdiction over you.

To constitute personal service the process must
be served on the defendant while he is physically
within the boundaries of the court's jurisdiction.
This is the usual way most lawsuits start; but not
always. Where a defendant is not in the state or
district he may still be served. Constructive service is usually accomplished by publication of copies
of the process in newspapers of general circulation,
or posting copies in public places. Substituted service is by mailing of process to the defendant at
his last known address. This term is also applied
where process is personally served on a defendant
who is outside the state.

A defendant may voluntarily consent to appear
in another jurisdiction, and such appearance is
sufficient, but a defendant may also make a "Special
Appearance" in most courts to fight jurisdiction.
Most states have "long arm statutes" which permits
jurisdiction over persons who "transact any business,
or commits a tortious act, or breaches a contract
within the state." The modern trend is for the states

to expand the application of these statutes to cover all situations "not inconsistent with the Constitution." At this time (1978) a case is pending in the U.S. Supreme Court on the constitutionality of these statutes. Most "long arm statutes" require personal service on the defendant outside the state, or at least, registered mail with return receipt requested. For example, California allows service by any form of airmail requiring a return receipt; or in any manner prescribed by the law of the place where the person is served. CCP 415.10, 40.

2. In Rem Jurisdiction

Where a plaintiff seeks a determination of rights in particular real or personal property, the court need have only in rem jurisdiction--judicial power over the property--the "res"--thing--involved. This gives the court power to decide the rights of all persons in the world having any interest in the property--regardless of whether they are subject to the personal jurisdiction of the court. Typically, this involves title to real or personal property, liens, foreclosures, and the like.

3. Subject Matter Jurisdiction

Subject matter jurisdiction simply relates to whether a particular court, under the statutes and laws, is the right court to decide the particular controversy. For example, you can't go to a probate court to decide "divorce" cases; a "domestic relations" court can't decide probate matters, etc. You can generally get all this information from the court clerks.

D. Venue

"Venue" refers to the proper place for trial of a lawsuit. In state courts the question usually is which county in the state is the proper place for trial; in federal courts--which judicial district.

Statutes regulating venue vary from state to state. In general, the codes provide that the proper court for trial of "transitory" actions is in the county in which any defendant resides. Special statutes frequently make other counties also proper for trial of certain kinds of cases, for example, personal injury cases in the county where the accident occurs; contract actions in the county where the contract was entered into or to be performed.

The venue for "local" actions is always the county where the property is located. And in a few states the policy that litigation involving local land be heard locally is so strong that venue is deemed a jurisdictional requirement as to certain

kinds of actions, that is, that the action must be
commenced there.

Proceedings to change venue are costly and often
cause a delay in bringing the matter to trial. For
this reason, some state codes authorize the court to
award reasonable expenses and attorney's fees to the
prevailing party in such proceedings. Some statutes
also stipulate that the expenses and fees must be
paid by the attorney for the losing party in the venue
proceedings out of his own pocket. This is an obvious
over reaction to the practice of lawyers taking such
measures to "delay" cases.

CHAPTER III

RULES OF COURT

A. How To Use The Court Rules

In representing yourself in any court action
the first thing you must have is a copy of the court
rules--the general court rules--and a copy of any
"local" court rules. Make sure you understand that
there are usually two sets of rules--and that you
get a copy of both. In the federal courts the general
court rules are called Federal Rules of Civil Procedure.
Most Federal District Courts have a separate set of
local rules which you must follow--to stay in court!

In state courts the general court rules are called
by various names including Rules of Court, Rules of
Civil Procedure, Civil Rules of Procedure, Court Rules,
Civil Code, Civil Procedure, Courts and Proceedings
in Civil Cases, Rules, Civil Practice and Procedure,
Courts and Civil Procedure, Rules of Procedure, and
other similar name tags. These are generally the
courts of general jurisdiction. The state courts of
limited jurisdiction usually have their own special
rules.

Each state generally has these rules in its

statute books or special rule books or both, except
that some of the courts of limited jurisdiction may
be in separate volumes. They are easy to find in any
law library, but if you have a case in court you need
your own copies. The Federal rules are used as a
model or pattern for the state rules, therefore we
will review in principle the federal rules to discuss
the most important items you need to know. The federal
rules were recently liberalized in certain "discovery"
procedures, therefore, we will use typical state rules
in discussing discovery procedures. Many of the states
have the same numbering system as the federal rules--
but not all. The few differences--or variations--will
be mentioned, but you must, in all events, get a copy
of your own court rules if you have, or will have, a
pending case.

Every application to the court for an order must
be made by motion or petition which should be in writing
unless made during a hearing or trial. The written
motion serves as notice to one's adversary and also
serves the function of preserving a written record of
the proceedings.

The basic parts of pleadings are:
1. Caption (court, file number, parties names).
2. Introductory clause (what the pleading is).

3. Body (allegations).
4. Demand for judgment or other relief (what you want).
5. Signature (by attorney or the individual party).
6. Certificate of service (except complaint and summons).

A certificate of service is not appropriate on a complaint or other original papers because they have to be served on the defendant.

Most court rules start with the pronouncement in Rule 1 that the purpose of the rules is to effect "the just, speedy and inexpensive determination of litigation."

Basically a "civil action" is resolve a controversy between parties and the purpose of pleadings is to develop the material issues of law and fact upon which to resolve the controversy.

Motions need not necessarily be on a separate piece of paper; you can put several in one document in most courts. You need to send a copy of all pleadings to the other parties and the typical certificate of service is:

I hereby certify that a copy hereof has been furnished to (party or his lawyer)   by (delivery, mail) this ____ day of_____, 1978.

_____
Your Name

Some local rules require the filing of written briefs

or authorities upon which the party relies. This can be very short. Do not argue in your motions--argue strongly in your legal briefs. If it is necessary to verify a pleading the usual form is:

Before me, the undersigned authority, this day personally appeared_____, who was sworn and says:_____.

Sworn to and subscribed before me on the_____day of_____, 1978.

(Notary Seal)   <u>Notary Public</u>

Pleadings under federal rules and most state rules include:

Plaintiff's Pleadings	Defendant's Pleadings
Complaint	Rule 12 Motions; Answer which may contain either counterclaim against Plaintiff or cross-claim against a co-defendant
Reply to counterclaim	
Answer to cross-claim	Third Party Complaint

In some state courts the pleadings allowed are:

Complaint	Demurrer; Answer
Demurrer to Answer	Cross-Complaint
Demurrer to Cross-Complaint	
Answer to Cross-Complaint	Demurrer to Answer to Cross-Complaint

See, for example, California CCP 422.10.

Offensive pleadings are those which set forth a claim for relief; defensive pleadings are statements of defenses. Complaint is a claim asserted by a plaintiff against a defendant; counter-claim is a claim asserted by a defendant against a plaintiff. Cross-claim is a claim by a defendant against a co-defendant or other party in the action. Third Party Complaint is a claim asserted by a defendant against one who is not a party to the original action which is, or may be, liable to the defendant for all or a part of the plaintiff's claim against the defendant.

Most court rules provide that a pleading which sets forth a claim for relief, whether an original claim, counterclaim, cross-claim, or third party claim, shall contain (1) a short and plain statement of the grounds upon which the court's jurisdiction depends, (2) a short and plain statement of the claim showing that the pleader is entitled to relief, and (3) a demand for judgment for the relief to which he deems himself entitled. Relief in the alternative or of several different types may be demanded. Averments shall be simple, concise, and direct. All pleadings shall be so construed as to do substantial justice.

Averments in a pleading to which a responsive pleading is required, other than those as to the amount of damage, are admitted when not denied in the responsive pleading. Averments in a pleading to which no responsive pleading is required or permitted shall be taken as denied or avoided. Read your court rules carefully on these points.

The pleadings prescribed in the court rules are merely one stage in the issue-narrowing process; discovery devices and pre-trial conferences are also available. The modern trend in all court rules is to liberalize the rules of pleading and streamline the pleading process so as to assure a determination of the litigation promptly and on the merits. At least, this is what the rule makers say.

B.   What Is A Cause of Action?

A cause of action is generally defined as the fact or facts which establish or give rise to a right of action, the existence of which affords a party a right to judicial relief. It is the right a party has to institute a judicial proceeding. A cause of action is that single group of facts which is claimed to have brought about an unlawful injury to the plaintiff and which entitles him to relief.

In common parlance a cause of action is frequently referred to as action, suit, case, cause, proceeding, lawsuit or a right "to sue the bastards." Under the modern court rules technical forms of action or technical remedies have been abolished and in most states there is but one form of action in civil suits, known as "civil action."

A right of action, or the plaintiff's right to sue, is determined or affected by three considerations.

1. There must be a cause of action.

2. All conditions precedent to bringing the suit must be performed.

3. There must not be a defense or bar to the maintenance of the suit.

The textbooks state it this way: the essential elements of a good cause of action are the existence of a legal right in the plaintiff, with a corresponding legal duty in the defendant, and a violation or breach of that right or duty, with consequential injury or damage to the plaintiff, for which he may maintain an action for recovery of money damages, or other appropriate relief.

C. How To Use The Forms In This Book

The forms listed in this book are primarily for illustration purposes, however, when used along with the form books cited in the Appendix, you will be able to take care of all your needs. The headings on the forms are examples only and you should check carefully

to make sure you get the correct names and numbers
on your pleadings. Most court rules provide that in
the caption of the summons and in the caption of the
complaint all parties must be named but in other
pleadings and papers, it is sufficient to state the
name of the first party on either side, with an
appropriate indication of other parties. For example,
John Doe, et al, v. ABC Corp, et al.

Some courts require a jurisdictional allegation;
some do not. Check your statutes and talk with your
court clerk.

Each pleading, motion, and other paper should be
signed by at least one attorney of record, in his
individual name, with his address and telephone number.
If a party is not represented by an attorney, the signature, address and telephone number of the party (pro
se) should be used. In all events the name and address
of the plaintiff should be shown on the complaint and
the name and address of the defendant should be shown
on the answer. This is to furnish a proper address
for service if an appeal is later filed.

The complaint in Form 3 has more counts than the
average lawsuit, but these are included to give you
more examples. The names, addresses and titles are
fictitious and the facts are hypothetical and are used
for illustration purposes only.

Your court rules will probably have examples of forms to be used in your court. Most state rules and rule books contain a long list of official forms for use in that court. You can't go wrong if you use the official court forms. Be sure to review your own court rules and forms before filing your pleadings.

D. How To Start Your Lawsuits: Commencement of Action

1. Getting It Filed

Most all the court rules provide that a civil action is commenced by filing a complaint with the court. The complaint must set forth the name of the court, the number assigned to the action (get this from the clerk), the designation of the pleading (usually just "Complaint" or "Complaint For Damages," etc.), and the name of the parties. A filing fee is always required.

2. Issuance of Summons and Service of Process

There is a specific rule on Process and Service of Process. This rule provides that upon the filing of a complaint the clerk shall forthwith issue a summons. It specifies that service of process shall be made by a United States Marshal, by his deputy, or by some person specially appointed by the court for that purpose. Most state courts permit the sheriff, deputy sheriff or any adult not interested in the suit to serve process. Generally personal service is made by delivery of the summons and complaint to the defendant personally, or by leaving copies thereof at his dwelling house or usual place of abode with some person of suitable age and discretion then residing therein or by delivering a copy of the summons and of the complaint to an agent authorized by appointment or by law to receive service of process.

There are specific methods for service of process on corporations, partnerships, associations, the government, a party not an inhabitant of, or found within, the state, and others. Check your court rules on this procedure.

Constitutional due process of law (14th Amendment to the U.S. Constitution) requires various standards in giving notice and an opportunity to defend. In a few state courts the action is commenced by the service of a summons before the complaint is filed.

3. Service and Filing of Pleadings and Other Papers

The general practice in most courts is to require that the original copy of a pleading (and sometimes one carbon copy) be filed with the court clerk, and that one copy be sent to each party to the action. Be sure to check your local rules because they frequently require that a supporting brief or memorandum of law be filed to support your motions.

    4. Time and Computation of Time

    The usual provision for computing any period of
time prescribed or allowed by the rules, is that the
day of the act, event, or default from which the designated period of time begins to run shall not be
included. The last day of the period so computed
shall be included, unless it is a Saturday, a Sunday,
or a legal holiday, in which event the period runs
until the end of the next day which is not a Saturday,
a Sunday, or a legal holiday. Legal holidays generally
include New Years Day, Washington's Birthday, Memorial
Day, Thanksgiving Day, Christmas Day, Independence Day,
Labor Day, Columbus Day, Veteran's Day.

    The court may, of course, upon timely motion
enlarge the time periods set out in the rules. This
is an easy way to delay any proceeding--if you have
a good reason to ask for an extension of time to file.
Most judges will routinely grant your first request.
Lawyers ask all the time. Moreover, most lawyers on
the other side will voluntarily agree to extensions
for almost any--or no--reason. After all why should
they be in a hurry? If you get friendly with the
lawyer for your adversary, you can probably delay him--
voluntarily--for years. He will, of course, have some
occasion to ask you for a "delay."

Form 1: Summons

IN THE UNITED STATES DISTRICT COURT

IN AND FOR THE SOUTHERN

DISTRICT OF CALIFORNIA

Civil Action Number____

JOHN DOE,   )

    Plaintiff   )

    v.   )   SUMMONS

RICHARD ROE,   )

    Defendant   )

You are hereby summoned and required to serve

upon_____, plaintiff's attorney, whose

address is_____, an answer to the

complaint which is herewith served upon you, within

_____days after service of this summons upon you,

exclusive of the day of service. If you fail to do

so, judgment by default will be taken against you for

the relief demanded in the complaint.

    Seal of Court   _____

                           Clerk of Court

    Date:_____

Form 2: Allegations of Jurisdiction

    a. Jurisdiction founded on diversity of citizen-
ship and amount--Federal Court

IN THE UNITED STATES DISTRICT COURT

IN AND FOR THE SOUTHERN

DISTRICT OF CALIFORNIA

Civil Action Number_____

JOHN DOE,   )

    Plaintiff   )

    v.   )   COMPLAINT

RICHARD ROE,   )

    Defendant   )

Plaintiff is a citizen of the State of A and
defendant is a corporation, incorporated under the
laws of the State of B -- having its principal place
of business in the State of B. The matter in controversy exceeds, exclusive of interest and costs,
the sum of ten thousand dollars.

    Seal of Court

                                    _____

    Date:_____   Clerk of Court

Form 3: Allegations of Jurisdiction

     b. Jurisdiction founded on the existence of
         a Federal Question--Federal Court

IN THE UNITED STATES DISTRICT COURT

IN AND FOR THE SOUTHERN

DISTRICT OF CALIFORNIA

Civil Action Number_____

JOHN DOE,	)	
Plaintiff	)	
v.	)	COMPLAINT
RICHARD ROE,	)	
Defendant	)	

This action arises under the Fourteenth Amendment
of the U.S. Constitution, Section 1, and 42 U.S.C.
1983, as hereafter more fully appears. The matter in
controversy exceeds, exclusive of interest and costs,
the sum of ten thousand dollars.

    Seal of Court

    Date:_____   _____
                                 Clerk of Court

Form 4: Allegations of Jurisdiction

    c. Jurisdiction allegations in state courts of limited jurisdiction--amounts

IN THE DISTRICT COURT IN AND

FOR ANYWHERE COUNTY

STATE OF ANYWHERE

Civil Action No_____

JOHN DOE,	)	
Plaintiff	)	
v.	)	COMPLAINT
RICHARD ROE,	)	
Defendant	)	

This action is based on a claim which does not exceed the sum of five thousand dollars, and is within the jurisdictional limits of this court.

Form 5:   Complaint

IN THE DISTRICT COURT IN AND

FOR ANYWHERE COUNTY

STATE OF ANYWHERE

Civil Action No____

JOHN DOE,   )
)
        Plaintiff   )
)
        v.   )   COMPLAINT
)
RICHARD ROE,   )
)
        Defendant   )

COUNT I   (Promissory Note)

1.   Defendant on or about July 1, 1977, executed
and delivered to plaintiff a promissory note, copy
of which is attached hereto as Exhibit A, whereby the
defendant promised to pay to plaintiff or order on
July 1, 1978, the sum of $1000 with interest thereon
at the rate of 10 percent per annum.

2.   Defendant owes to plaintiff the amount of
said note and interest plus attorney's fees.

Wherefore, plaintiff demands judgment against the
defendant for the sum of $1000 plus interest, court
costs, expenses, and attorney's fees.

Form 5: Complaint (continued)

COUNT II (Account)

3. Defendant owes plaintiff $1000 according to the account attached hereto as Exhibit B.

Wherefore plaintiff demands judgment against the defendant for the sum of $1000 plus interest, court costs, expenses, and attorney's fees.

COUNT III (Negligence)

4. On July 1, 1977, on a public highway called First Street in City, State, defendant negligently drove a motor vehicle against plaintiff who was then crossing said highway.

5. As a result plaintiff was thrown down and had his leg broken and was otherwise injured, was prevented from transacting his business, suffered great pain of body and mind, and incurred expenses for medical attention and hospitalization in the sum of $1000.

Wherefore plaintiff demands judgment against defendant in the sum of $50,000 plus interests, court costs, expenses and attorney's fees.

John Doe
123 First Street
City, State
300-123-4567
In Pro Per

E. How You (as defendant) Can Attack A Complaint

Before filing an answer to the complaint the defendant may challenge the legal sufficiency of the complaint--why not? It takes a long time! There is a full arsenal of pleadings you can use to run the other side and his attorney ragged! Lawyers frequently refer to these motions as "Rule 12 Motions." Everybody around the court house knows what that term means. Delay!

Because of its importance to you Rule 12 of the Federal Rules (also Rule 12 in most state rules) is quoted in full. Study it carefully, and use it to the ultimate.

Rule 12. Defenses and Objections--When and How Presented--By Pleading or Motion--Motion for Judgment on Pleadings

(a) When Presented. A defendant shall serve his answer within 20 days after the service of the summons and complaint upon him, except when service is made under Rule 4(e) and a different time is prescribed in the order of court under the statute of the United States or in the statute or rule of court of the state. A party served with a pleading stating a cross-claim against him shall serve an answer thereto within 20 days after the service upon him. The plaintiff shall serve his reply to a counterclaim in the answer within 20 days after service of the answer or, if a reply is ordered by the court, within 20 days after service of the order, unless the order otherwise directs. The United States or an officer or agency thereof shall serve an answer to the complaint or to a cross-claim, or a reply to a counterclaim, within 60 days after the service upon the United States attorney

of the pleading in which the claim is asserted.
The service of a motion permitted under this
rule alters these periods of time as follows,
unless a different time is fixed by order of
the court: (1) if the court denies the motion
or postpones its disposition until the trial
on the merits, the responsive pleading shall
be served within 10 days after notice of the
court's action; (2) if the court grants a motion
for a more definite statement the responsive
pleading shall be served within 10 days after
the service of the more definite statement.

(b) How Presented. Every defense, in law or
fact, to a claim for relief in any pleading,
whether a claim, counterclaim, cross-claim,
or third-party claim, shall be asserted in the
responsive pleading thereto if one is required,
except that the following defenses may at the
option of the pleader be made by motion: (1)
lack of jurisdiction over the subject matter,
(2) lack of jurisdiction over the person, (3)
improper venue, (4) insufficiency of process,
(5) insufficiency of service of process, (6)
failure to state a claim upon which relief can
be granted, (7) failure to join a party under
Rule 19. A motion making any of these defenses
shall be made before pleading if a further
pleading is permitted. No defense or objection
is waived by being joined with one or more other
defenses or objections in a responsive pleading
or motion. If a pleading sets forth a claim
for relief to which the adverse party is not
required to serve a responsive pleading, he
may assert at the trial any defense in law or
fact to that claim for relief. If, on a motion
asserting the defense numbered (6) to dismiss
for failure of the pleading to state a claim
upon which relief can be granted, matters outside the pleading are presented to and not
excluded by the court, the motion shall be
treated as one for summary judgment and disposed
of as provided in Rule 56, and all parties shall
be given reasonable opportunity to present all
material made pertinent to such a motion by Rule
56.

(c) Motion for Judgment on the Pleadings. After
the pleadings are closed but within such time as
not to delay the trial, any party may move for
judgment on the pleadings. If, on a motion for
judgment on the pleadings, matters outside the
pleadings are presented to and not excluded by
the court, the motion shall be treated as one
for summary judgment and disposed of as provided in Rule 56, and all parties shall be given
reasonable opportunity to present all material
made pertinent to such a motion by Rule 56.

(d) Preliminary Hearings. The defenses specifically enumerated (1)-(7) in subdivision (b)
of this rule, whether made in a pleading or by
motion, and the motion for judgment mentioned
in subdivision (c) of this rule shall be heard
and determined before trial on application of
any party, unless the court orders that the
hearing and determination thereof be deferred
until the trial.

(e) Motion for More Definite Statement. If a
pleading to which a responsive pleading is permitted is so vague or ambiguous that a party
cannot reasonably be required to frame a responsive pleading, he may move for a more definite
statement before interposing his responsive
pleading. The motion shall point out the defects
complained of and the details desired. If the
motion is granted and the order of the court
is not obeyed within 10 days after notice of
the order or within such other time as the
court may fix, the court may strike the pleading to which the motion was directed or make
such order as it deems just.

(f) Motion to Strike. Upon motion made by a
party before responding to a pleading or, if
no responsive pleading is permitted by these
rules, upon motion made by a party within 20
days after the service of the pleading upon
him or upon the court's own initiative at any
time, the court may order stricken from any
pleading any insufficient defense or any redundant, immaterial, impertinent, or scandalous
matter.

(g)   Consolidation of Defenses in Motion.   A
party who makes a motion under this rule may
join with it any other motions herein provided
for and then available to him.   If a party makes
a motion under this rule but omits therefrom any
defense or objection then available to him which
this rule permits to be reised by motion, he
shall not thereafter make a motion based on the
defense or objection so omitted, except a motion
as provided in subdivision (h)(2) hereof on any
of the grounds there stated.

(h)   Waiver or Preservation of Certain Defenses.
   (1)   A defense of lack of jurisdiction over
   the person, improper venue, insufficiency of
   process, or insufficiency of service of process is waived (A) if omitted from a motion
   in the circumstances described in subdivision (g), or (B) if it is neither made by
   motion under this rule nor included in a
   responsive pleading or an amendment thereof
   permitted by Rule 15(a) to be made as a matter
   of course.
   (2)   A defense of failure to state a claim
   upon which relief can be granted, a defense
   of failure to join a party indispensable
   under Rule 19, and an objection of failure
   to state a legal defense to a claim may be
   made in any pleading permitted or ordered
   under Rule 7(a), or by motion for judgment
   on the pleadings, or at the trial on the
   merits.
   (3)   Whenever it appears by suggestion of
   the parties or otherwise that the court lacks
   jurisdiction of the subject matter, the court
   shall dismiss the action.

Where a defendant files a motion "permitted

under this rule" it alters the period of time for

filing your answer!   And who's in a hurry?   Let's

talk about these "Rule 12 Motions."   They are more

fun than a toy pistol and more effective that a

double barreled shotgun.

1. How To File A Motion To Dismiss

This motion may be called a "demurrer" in some
state rules. It is the same thing. In testing the
sufficiency of a complaint under Rule 12 motions the
court will construe it in the light most favorable
to the plaintiff. The plaintiff need only state a
claim upon which relief may be granted--he need not
state facts about his evidence. The sufficiency of
the complaint is determined from the facts pleaded
and reasonable inferences to be drawn from them.

If you attack the lack of jurisdiction, insufficiency of process or service of process you may
need to file an affidavit to give the judge evidence
to support your point. For example, if the deputy
sheriff left the summons and complaint with your neigh-
bor instead of you or your family, you should file an
affidavit to prove your facts to the judge.

In preparing your motion to dismiss use the forms
in this book and other form books, but be sure to use
only those grounds that you have some support for.
Lawyers as a matter of course frequently file a motion
to dismiss on the broad, sweeping grounds of "failure
to state a cause of action" no matter how "good" the
complaint may be, and judges condone it. It is a habit
lawyers have to get delays.

If the judge grants your motion to dismiss for failure to state a cause of action he will almost always let the plaintiff amend at least one time-- and usually more. Of course, this takes a lot of time. If your motion is denied you then proceed to file your answer, but only after all Rule 12 motions have been ruled on by the court.

2. Filing Your Motion For More Definite Statement

This is called a Bill of Particulars in some states. Because of the liberal construction of the "simple" statement rule most courts won't grant this motion--but most complaints are vague or ambiguous. And this always gives you a good shot at convincing the judge to grant your motion. As a safety measure you should flood the plaintiff with a load of written interrogatories about the facts alleged in his complaint--and you generally get the answers under oath long before you ever have to file your answer to the complaint. And remember, when you file this motion don't bother to call it up for hearing, unless the rules require it. Maybe it will just set there forever.

Read the complaint against you, read the rule again, and state all the grounds available to you in support of your Motion For More Definite Statement.

3. Motion To Strike

Either party may move to strike any insufficient defense or any "redundant, immaterial, impertinent or scandalous" matter in the pleadings of the other party. Most judges don't like these motions, but if the other party gets a little nasty in his allegations give him a shot. Profane or repulsive language is generally improper in a pleading. Moreover, in some courts a party is permitted to read the pleadings to the jury at the trial. In those courts you should flood the other side with motions to strike. In those courts you can also read the other guy's pleadings to the jury in those courts that permit it. Look at some of the cases in the annotations to your court rules to get some good ideas about what grounds the judges usually grant.

4. Procedures In Preparing and Filing Your Motions

Rule 12 motions must be in writing and must specify the ground or grounds upon which they are based. In other words tell the judge the reasons you are relying on. Always file the motions within the 20 or 30 days stated in the summons; and check your local rules about filing briefs.

5. Don't Waive Any Defenses By Neglecting To State Them All In Your First Motion

When you file a Rule 12 motion include all defenses permitted and also file all of the motions you plan to use under Rule 12 otherwise they are waived; except the following basic defenses are never waived and can be raised at any time: lack of jurisdiction over the subject matter, failure to join an indespensible party; and failure to state a claim upon which relief can be granted (or failure to state a cause of action). It is a good idea to read the rule again to make sure you've got this point.

6. How To Get A Hearing On Your Motions-- If You Want One

The local procedures vary as to how a party arranges to have his motions ruled on by the judge. In some courts the judge may rule without a hearing. In most courts one of the parties has to check with the clerk, the judge's secretary, the judge's clerk, or some other court official to arrange for a hearing. Check your local rules. In some courts there is an old fashioned procedure to file a formal "notice" of a time to appear in court to get an appointment. Of course, when you file a Rule 12 motion--unless the local rules require it--you do not <u>have</u> to arrange to call them up for hearing. In other words where the rules do not require it (and most do not) you can just

let the motion set there--forever--and unless the
lawyer for the other side arranges for a hearing, you
can let it stay in status quo forever. Why do you
think it takes lawyers so long to get cases to trial?
I have seen many lawsuits dismissed for lack of prosecution where neither party (or the lawyers) bothered
to schedule a hearing on pending motions. Moreover,
I have seen many lawyers let a case hang in suspension--
while telling their clients, "I can't do anything
until the judge rules on the pending motions." Little
did the client know he had a lazy--or stupid--lawyer.
I have also prosecuted many "disciplinary" proceedings
(for the bar association) and presided over such disciplinary proceedings (as a member of ethics committees)
where lawyers failed to arrange for hearings on pending
motions--and told the client he was waiting for the
"judge" to act! The burden of what I am saying is that
you will find _many_ lawyers who will let motions hang
forever--let's say they are "too busy" to arrange for
hearings.

It is a good idea to get on good terms with the
court personnel and you can discover many procedural
advantages in handling your own case--and a million
ways to delay. They have seen all of them!

Form 6: Motion To Dismiss

IN THE DISTRICT COURT IN AND

FOR ANYWHERE COUNTY

STATE OF ANYWHERE

Civil Action No____

JOHN DOE,   )
)
    Plaintiff   )
)
    v.   )   MOTION TO DISMISS
)
RICHARD ROE,   )
)
    Defendant   )

Defendant moves for the entry of an order dis-
missing the complaint on the following grounds:

    1. The complaint fails to state a claim against
defendant upon which relief can be granted in that:
(here insert the specific grounds on which the court
should dismiss the action).

    2. Lack of jurisdiction over the subject matter
in that_____(state specific grounds).

    3. Lack of jurisdiction over the person in that

_____.

    4. Insufficiency of process in that_____.

    5. Insufficiency of service of process in that

_____.

Form 4:   Motion To Dismiss (continued)

6.   Failure to join an indispensible party, it affirmatively appearing from the allegations of the complaint that_____(state the specific grounds).

I hereby certify that a copy hereof was mailed to_____on the_____day of_____.

Your Name
Address
Phone Number
In Pro Per

Form 7: Motion To Strike

IN THE DISTRICT COURT IN AND

FOR ANYWHERE COUNTY

STATE OF ANYWHERE

Civil Action No____

JOHN DOE,	)	
Plaintiff	)	
v.	)	MOTION TO STRIKE
RICHARD ROE,	)	
Defendant	)	

Defendant moves for the entry of an order striking the following parts of the complaint on the grounds that they are redundant, immaterial, impertinent and scandalous:

1.

2.

3.

(Certificate of Service)   (Signature)

Form 8: Motion For More Definite Statement

                    IN THE DISTRICT COURT IN AND

                        FOR ANYWHERE COUNTY

                          STATE OF ANYWHERE
                          Civil Action No____

JOHN DOE,   )
)
     Plaintiff   )
)   MOTION FOR MORE
     v.   )   DEFINITE STATEMENT
)
RICHARD ROE,   )
)
     Defendant   )

Defendant moves for a more definite statement of
the following:

     1.

     2.

because each of them is so vague and ambiguous that
defendant cannot reasonably frame a responsive pleading.

          (Certificate of Service)   (Signature)

Form 9: Motion For Judgment On Pleadings

                    IN THE DISTRICT COURT IN AND

                        FOR ANYWHERE COUNTY

                          STATE OF ANYWHERE
                          Civil Action No____

JOHN DOE,   )
)
        Plaintiff   )
)   MOTION FOR JUDGMENT
        v.   )
)   ON PLEADINGS
RICHARD ROE,   )
)
        Defendant   )

Defendant moves for a judgment on the pleadings.

(Certificate of Service)   (Signature)

Form 10: Notice of Hearing

                    IN THE DISTRICT COURT IN AND

                        FOR ANYWHERE COUNTY

                          STATE OF ANYWHERE
                          Civil Action No____

JOHN DOE,   )
)
        Plaintiff   )
)
        v.   )   NOTICE OF HEARING
)
RICHARD ROE,   )
)
        Defendant   )

        Notice is hereby given that defendant will call

up for hearing the Motion To Dismiss before the Honor-

able Roy Bean in his chambers in the Royal County

Courthouse, 888 First Street, City, State, on the

15th day of June, 1978, at 10 A.M. or as soon there-

after as the parties may be heard.

        (Certificate of Service)   (Signature

Form 11: Order Granting Motion To Dismiss

IN THE DISTRICT COURT IN AND

FOR ANYWHERE COUNTY

STATE OF ANYWHERE

Civil Action No____

JOHN DOE,   )
)
        Plaintiff   )
)
        v.   )   ORDER GRANTING
)   MOTION TO DISMISS
RICHARD ROE,   )
)
        Defendant   )

This action was heard on defendant's motion to
dismiss the complaint, and it is

ADJUDGED as follows:

1. The complaint is dismissed.

2. Plaintiff shall have 20 days from this date
within which to file and serve an Amended Complaint,
and defendant shall have 20 days after service of the
Amended Complaint within which to respond.

Done and Ordered this____day of June, 1978, at
City, State.

                              _____
                              District Judge

F. How To Prepare Your Answer and Defenses--
    When You Are Defendant

Your answer tells the plaintiff what you deny in
his complaint, and what "goodies" you have lined up
for him by way of defenses--or alleged defenses. It
is good practice for you to respond separately to the
numbered paragraphs of the complaint and unequivocally
deny or admit each allegation. If you don't deny some
allegations they may be deemed admitted. It is generally poor and sloppy practice to deny everything
(general denial) in the complaint--it can't be that
bad--can it? It is good practice to admit truthful
allegations that are easy to prove. For example, if
the plaintiff alleges that he is "over the age of 21,"
and lives at a certain address, you'd probably admit
that.

The rules require good faith in pleadings. But
ambiguous, uncertain, or vague allegations shouldn't
slip by you, especially if they are hard for the
plaintiff to prove. And you don't have to admit
essential elements of plaintiff's cause of action
that are couched in conclusions--he has to prove it!
For example, here's a story I like to tell about my
wife: she got a traffic ticket for failure to stop
at a stop sign. She didn't stop! I went to court
with her and when the judge said, "How do you plead?"

I said, "Not Guilty." My wife looked up at me, surprised, and said, very seriously, "But that's lying, isn't it?" I had to explain to her that under the laws and the constitutions a person doesn't have to convict themselves--the prosecutor has to prove it.

Same with civil litigation. If plaintiff alleged I owed him $100 and I file an answer and "admit" it, he is automatically entitled to a judgment. Your testimony under oath about "facts" and evidence is different, but you can certainly deny conclusions alleged in plaintiff's complaint. For example, you may "admit" you borrowed $100 from plaintiff, but "deny" you owe him $100. Who knows how many defenses you may "discover" in your court proceedings and discovery. In all events you can put a plaintiff to his proof. But, remember, when you are a plaintiff the defendant can do the same thing to you. Have your evidence ready before trial.

After responding separately--and carefully-- to the allegations of the complaint you should then affirmatively state any of the specific defenses you may have--or be entitled to assert--under the rules-- or otherwise.

Affirmative defenses involve "new matter" which must be pleaded in the answer--and proven at trial--

to avoid the plaintiff's claims. You may waive your defenses if you don't plead them in your answer. You always have the burden of proof on these issues. For example, you may admit you owed the plaintiff $1000 (once upon a time), but plead that the statute of limitations is a bar to the action. If the statute of limitations has run on the claim he can't collect a dime from you. And look at all the other possible defenses listed below.

In order to emphasize the importance of the af-firmative defenses listed in most of the court rules, they are reported here for your convenience:

        Accord and Satisfaction
        Arbitration and Award
        Assumption of Risk
        Contributory Negligence
        Discharge in Bankruptcy
        Duress
        Estoppel
        Failure of Consideration
        Fraud
        Illegality
        Injury by Fellow Servant
        Laches
        License
        Payment
        Release
        Res Judicata
        Statute of Frauds
        Statute of Limitations
        Waiver
        Others

See definitions in Glossary.

If, when you file your answer, you are uncertain about whether you have evidence or facts to support a defense plead it anyway. Find the evidence later. Don't lose a good defense by failing to assert it in your answer even though you are permitted under the rules to move to have the judge authorize an amendment to your pleadings. Who knows you may find some evidence to support them. Like duress, fraud, and the like. At least you can ask the plaintiff about it in written interrogatories. And who's in a hurry?

G. How To Plead Your Counterclaims and Cross-Claims

Rule 13. Counterclaim and Cross-Claim
(a) Compulsory Counterclaims. A pleading shall state as a counterclaim any claim which at the time of serving the pleading the pleader has against any opposing party, if it arises our of the transaction or occurrence that is the subject matter of the opposing party's claim and does not require for its adjudication the presence of third parties of whom the court cannot acquire jurisdiction. But the pleader need not state the claim if (1) at the time the action was commenced the claim was the subject of another pending action, or (2) the opposing party brought suit upon his claim by attachment or other process by which the court did not acquire jurisdiction to render a personal judgment on that claim, and the pleader is not stating any counterclaim under this Rule 13.

(b) Permissive Counterclaims. A pleading may state as a counterclaim any claim against an opposing party not arising out of the transaction or occurrence that is the subject matter of the opposing party's claim.

(c)   Counterclaim Exceeding Opposing Claim.   A counterclaim may or may not diminish or defeat the recovery sought by the opposing party.   It may claim relief exceeding in amount or different in kind from that sought in the pleading of the opposing party.

(d)   Counterclaim Against the United States. These rules shall not be construed to enlarge beyond the limits now fixed by law the right to assert counterclaims or to claim credits against the United States or an officer or agency thereof.

(e)   Counterclaim Maturing or Acquired After Pleading.   A claim which either matured or was acquired by the pleader after serving his pleading may, with the permission of the court, be presented as a counterclaim by supplemental pleading.

(f)   Omitted Counterclaim.   When a pleader fails to set up a counterclaim through oversight, inadvertence, or excusable neglect, or when justice requires, he may by leave of court set up the counterclaim by amendment.

(g)   Cross-Claim Against Co-Party.   A pleading may state as a cross-claim any claim by one party against a co-party arising out of the transaction or occurrence that is the subject matter either of the original action or of a counterclaim therein or relating to any property that is the subject matter of the original action. Such cross-claim may include a claim that the party against whom it is asserted is or may be liable to the cross-claimant for all or part of a claim asserted in the action against the cross-claimant.

(h)   Joinder of Additional Parties.   Persons other than those made parties to the original action may be made parties to a counterclaim or cross-claim in accordance with the provisions of Rule 19 and 20.

(i)   Separate Trials; Separate Judgments.   If the court orders separate trials as provided in Rule 42(b), judgment on a counterclaim or cross-claim may be rendered in accordance with the terms of Rule 54(b) when the court has jurisdiction so to do, even if the claims of the opposing party have been dismissed or otherwise disposed of.

As a defendant you should first file your Rule 12 Motions. That takes a lot of time to get them resolved. You file your answer with any affirmative defenses you may have, or have. During this time you should be pounding away at the other side with written interrogatories, requests for admission of facts, motions to produce, etc. You are not finished yet! As long as you have been made a defendant in court you might as well sue the other guy for all claims you have against him. Your counterclaim may be related to the claims set forth in the complaint (compulsory counterclaim), or it may relate to some other transaction (permissive counterclaim). If your claim arises out of the same transaction or occurrence as that alleged in the complaint it is compulsory--you must file it now or lose it. If your claim is based on some independent ground (anything at all) it is permissive--you can counterclaim now--or sue later--at your option. But as long as you are there--why not give it a shot?

Now, after you consider your lawsuits against
the plaintiff you should consider suing any other
parties in the case--any co-defendants or co-plaintiffs.
This is done by a cross-claim--in the same suit. However, your cross-claim against a co-defendant must
relate to the "transaction or occurrence" alleged in
the complaint. Your answer, counterclaim and cross-
claim can all be in the same pleading in most courts.

H. Third Party Complaints

OK, you're not finished yet. In most courts a
defendant may sue some other person not a party to
the action who is or may be liable to him for all or
part of the plaintiff's claim against him. Thus a
controversy that otherwise would require more than
one action for final determination can be resolved
in one proceeding. The procedure is designed to save
time and expenses and to avoid differing results from
the same set of facts.

If a counterclaim is brought against the plaintiff,
he may also bring in a third party. So, after you
assert your defenses and claims against the plaintiff,
you should assert your claims against anybody else in
the whole world that may be liable or responsible in
any way. The more parties you get in the lawsuit (in
good faith) the more your chances are of getting out.

In some state courts the counterclaim, cross-claim, and third party complaint may not be recognized as such, but provisions are usually made for you to bring a separate action (called a cross complaint) against the plaintiff, a co-defendant or some third person not yet a party to the action. In these situations the judge will generally consolidate the cases which reaches the same results as the modern rules-- just one big happy family of litigants!

I. **Discovery:** The Procedural Tool By Which Both Plaintiffs and Defendants Get Facts and Evidence To Prepare For Trial

Now, here's where the real fun starts. We come to the difference between the allegata and the probata (latin for allegations and proof). All you need for making allegations is a piece of paper and a typewriter. When the troops gather down at the courthouse the guy with the "evidence," "facts," "proof," will carry the day. Proper use of discovery proceedings is the easy-- long--way to get it. If you use these techniques properly, you can find out every witness the other parties will call at the trial, all the testimony they have, all documents and records the other parties have and just about anything else you want to know about them. Anything that is relevant, or that may lead to the discovery of relevant evidence can be inquired into.

You can have the other side and their lawyers beat
to a frazzle before they recover from your pleadings
and discovery. Now do you see why it takes lawyers
so long to get cases to trial?

A discovery program has three practical purposes:

(1) To narrow the issues to those matters
     actually disputed;

(2) To secure information regarding the exist-
     ence of evidence that may or may not be
     used at trial; and

(3) To obtain evidence for use at trial.

The rules are designed to ensure against surprise,
trickery, bluff and legal gymnastics at trial and to
assist in achieving just results based on truth.

Informal discovery involves informal investigations,
interviews, research, study and physical inspection
outside the realm of formal discovery procedures under
court rules. You can have a good time being a detective--
being your own investigator.

Under the discovery rules you can generally get
any matter not priviledged, evidence relevant to the
subject matter of the suit, facts calculated to lead
to the discovery of admissible evidence, some work pro-
duct of the lawyers, and some opinions of experts.

The court discovery rules are so liberal now
that practically anything is discoverable. In fact

the federal rules were expanded just a few years ago
to make them even more liberal. Ironically, at the
time of this writing (1978) a Special Committee for
the Study of Discovery Abuse of the American Bar
Association Section of Litigation has just completed
action recommending reforms in nineteen subsections
of the Civil Rules of Procedure of the U.S. District
Courts. One recommendation would limit the scope
of discovery to material relevant to "issues raised
by the claims or defenses of any party." Most state
court rules have not yet adopted the new changes,
therefore we will use a sample of the state rules on
discovery--for our discussions--rather than the Federal Rules. In all events you should study your own
court rules and use them effectively.

There are five major tools under the rules for
discovery:

    (1) Depositions;

    (2) Written Interrogatories to Witnesses;

    (3) Written Interrogatories to Parties;

    (4) Motion to Produce Documents, etc.; and

    (5) Request For Admissions.

1. Depositions: Your First Discovery Weapon

This rule permits any party to take the testimony--
under oath--of any person, including a party, by

deposition upon oral examination. You can do this anytime after the summons and complaint have been served as long as you give the other parties and witnesses reasonable notice under the rules. It is a simple procedure--but relatively expensive as compared with the other tools you have available for discovery. You merely file in the court file--with a copy to all parties--a Notice of Taking Deposition stating the time and place and name and addresses of each person to be examined. You can also--under most court rules--require the other party to bring with him and produce designated documents, records, or other evidence you may want to examine, copy or ask questions about. If you depose a witness who is not a party to the action you have to arrange for him to voluntarily appear for the deposition or subpoena him. You don't have to subpoena a party. You must arrange for a court reporter (or other stenographer authorized to take depositions in your court to transcribe the testimony and arrange to pay the court reporter a "sitting" fee plus the cost of typing up the testimony (if you decide to type it up--usually not required). The reporters fee may be 25 to 50 dollars per day and the cost of typing the transcript is extra if you have the reporter prepare it. In some states you may also use videotapes instead of a court reporter. This is a good plan if you have the equipment available.

You put the party--or witness--under oath and proceed to ask him just about any questions you want that are relevant to the suit or counterclaims. Read your court rules on this topic very carefully to make sure you follow all the requirements. This is more complicated--and more expensive--than the written interrogatories to a party, discussed later. But, if you have a few hundred dollars you can put the other party through a ringer--as many times as the judge will let you.

2.   How To Reduce The Costs of Depositions

Here's a maneuver I have seen pulled a million times by a lawyer or party who wants to take the deposition of an adverse party--but not run up a bunch of fees and costs for a court reporter. I've done it a few times myself! Notice the adverse party for his deposition in your office. Instead of hiring a court reporter get your secretary (or wife) to "transcribe" the testimony. It doesn't matter if your secretary can't transcribe 5 words per minute--just have her set there with a pad and pencil and scratch very fast on her pad. Any person who is a notary can put the

witness under oath--or you may be able to do it your-
self--or let your secretary do it if no one challenges
it. Ask all the questions you want--relevant and
irrelevant--as many and as long as you like. If the
other party doesn't raise the question of the competency
of the "court reporter" it may be waived--at least you
get your information without the cost of a reporter.
If the other party raised any objection to the competency of the "reporter" you simply cancel the deposition and reschedule it at a later date. You can
do the same thing with other "witnesses" if you like.
It just depends on how brave you are. Don't be timid.
You can't be too forceful in the defense of yourself!

3. Depositions Upon Written Questions

This procedure is similar to the Deposition
rule, except that it is less expensive--takes more
time--and usually produces less evidence and is a
lot less fun. But, if you are short on funds for
discovery--and don't have the stomach for the old
"deposition without a court reporter" trick, study
this rule carefully and give it your best shot. But,
look at Rule 33, 34, and 36 first!

We're only just beginning. You have an incredible
arsenal for stirring things up in a lawsuit. Now, do
you know why lawyers take so long to get to the end of
a lawsuit?

4. Written Interrogatories to Parties: Your Best
   Discovery Weapon

Rule 33. Interrogatories to Parties
(a) Availability; Procedures for Use. Any party
may serve upon any other party written interrogatories to be answered by the party served or, if
the party served is a public or private corporation,
or a partnership, or association, or governmental
agency, by any officer or agent, who shall furnish
such information as is available to the party.
Interrogatories may, without leave of court, be
served upon the plaintiff after commencement of
the action and upon any other party with or
after service of the summons upon that party.

Each interrogatory shall be answered separately
and fully in writing under oath, unless it is
objected to, in which event the reasons for
objection shall be stated in lieu of an answer.
The answers are to be signed by the person making
them, and the objections signed by the attorney
making them. The party upon whom the interrogatories have been served shall serve a copy of
the answers, and objections if any, within 30
days after the service of the interrogatories,
except that a defendant may serve answers or
objections within 45 days after service of the
summons upon that defendant. The court may
allow a shorter or longer time. The party submitting the interrogatories may move for an order
under Rule 37 (a) with respect to any objection
to or other failure to answer an interrogatory.

(b) Scope; Use at Trial. Interrogatories may
relate to any matters used to the extent permitted
by the rules of evidence.

An interrogatory otherwise proper is not necessarily objectionable merely because an answer
to the interrogatory involves an opinion or con-
tention that relates to fact or the application
of law to fact, but the court may order that
such an interrogatory need not be answered until
after designated discovery has been completed or
until a pre-trial conference or other later time.

(c) Option to Produce Business Records. Where the answer to an interrogatory may be derived or ascertained from the business records of the party upon whom the interrogatory has been served, or from an examination, audit, or inspection of such business records, or from a compilation, abstract, or summary based thereon, and the burden of deriving or ascertaining the answer is substantially the same for the party serving the interrogatory as for the party served, it is a sufficient answer to such interrogatory to specify the records from which the answer may be derived or ascertained and to afford to the party serving the interrogatory reasonable opportunity to examine, audit, or inspect such records and to make copies, compilations, abstracts, or summaries.

This procedure is best for getting:

(1) Simple facts concerning background or foundational information, such as exact dates, witnesses, times and places;

(2) Admissions as to contentions that narrow or reduce issues;

(3) Exact names and addresses of persons and exact identification of relevant documents-- for further discovery;

(4) Specific facts supporting general allegations in pleadings or clarifying approximations in depositions; and

(5) Identification of trial experts and the substance of their opinions.

If the other party doesn't answer or is vague, evasive or ambiguous you can file a battery of motions, hearings and sanctions. Moreover, these little "procedural techniques" don't cost you any money and it takes a lot of time to finish it all. Give it a try; you can really enjoy doing this to the other side.

5. Production of Documents and Things

Rule 34. Production of Documents and Things and Entry Upon Land for Inspection and Other Purposes

(a) Scope. Any party may serve on any other party a request: (1) To produce and permit the party making the request, or someone acting on his behalf, to inspect and copy, any designated documents (including writtings, drawings, graphs, charts, photographs, phono-records, and other data compilations from which information can be obtained, translated, if necessary, by the respondent through detection devices into reasonably usable form), or to inspect and copy, test, or sample any tangible things which constitute or contain matters within the scope of Rule 26 (b) and which are in the possession, custody, or control of the party upon whom the request is served; or (2) to permit entry upon designated land or other property in the possession or control of the party upon whom the request is served for the purpose of inspection and measuring, surveying, photographing, testing, or sampling the property or any designated objection or operation thereon, within the scope of Rule 26 (b).

(b) Procedure. The request may, without leave of court, be served upon the plaintiff after commemcement of the action and upon any other party with or after service of the summons upon that party. The request shall set forth the items to be inspected either by individual item or by category, and describe each item and category with reasonable particularity. The request shall specify a reasonable time, place, and manner of making the inspection and performing the related acts.

The party upon whom the request is served shall serve a written response within 30 days after the service of the request, except that a defendant may serve a response within 45 days after service cf the summons upon that defendant. The court may allow a shorter or longer time. The response shall state, with respect to each item or category, that inspection and related activities will be permitted as requested, unless the request

is objected to, in which event the reasons for
objection shall be stated. If objection is
made to part of an item or category, the part
shall be specified. The party submitting the
request may move for an order under Rule 37
(a) with respect to any objection to or other
failure to respond to the request or any part
thereof, or any failure to permit inspection as
requested.

(c) Persons Not Parties. This rule does not
preclude an independent action against a person
not a party for production of documents and things
and permission to enter upon land.

This is another easy to use, inexpensive

discovery procedure you can use. Take a look

at the Rule and Forms and let your imagination

loose on the number of requests you can make

of the other parties.

6. Requests For Admission

Rule 36. Requests for Admission
A party may serve upon any other party a written
request for the admission, for purposes of the
pending action only, of the truth of any matters
within the scope of Rule 26 (b) set forth in the
request that relate to statements or opinions of
fact or of the application of law to fact, including the genuineness of any documents described in the request. Copies of documents
shall be served with the request unless they
have been or are otherwise furnished or made
available for inspection and copying. The
request may, without leave of court, be served
upon the plaintiff after commencement of the
action and upon any other party with or after
service of the summons upon that party.

Each matter of which an admission is requested
shall be separately set forth. The matter is
admitted unless, within 30 days after service
of the request, or within such shorter or

longer time as the court may allow, the party
to whom the request is directed serves upon the
party requesting the admission a written answer
or objection addressed to the matter, signed
by the party or by his attorney, but, unless
the court shortens the time, a defendant shall
not be required to serve answers or objections
before the expiration of 45 days after service
of the summons upon him. If objection is made,
the reasons therefor shall be stated. The
answer shall specifically deny the matter or
set forth in detail the reasons why the answering party cannot truthfully admit or deny the
matter. A denial shall fairly meet the substance
of the requested admission, and when good faith
requires that a party qualify his answer or deny
only a part of the matter of which an admission
is requested, he shall specify so much of it as
is true and qualify or deny the remainder. An
answering party may not give lack of information
or knowledge as a reason for faulure to admit or
deny unless he states that he has made reasonable
inquiry and that the information known or readily
obtainable by him is insufficient to enable him
to admit or deny. A party who considers that a
matter of which an admission has been requested
presents a genuine issue for trial may not, on
that ground alone, object to the request; he may,
subject to the provisions of Rule 37 (c), deny
the matter or set forth reasons why he cannot admit or deny it.

The party who has requested the admissions may
move to determine the sufficiency of the answer
or objections. Unless the court determines that
an objection is justified, it shall order that an
answer be served. If the court determines that
an answer does not comply with the requirements
of this Rule, it may order either that the matter
is admitted or that an amended answer be served.
The court may, in lieu of these orders, determine
that final disposition of the request be made at
a pre-trial conference or at a designated time
prior to trial. The provisions of Rule 37 (a)
(4) apply to the award of expenses incurred in
relation to the motion.

(b) Effect of Admission. Any matter admitted under this Rule is conclusively established unless the court on motion permits withdrawal or amendment of the admission. Subject to the provisions of Rule 16 governing amendment of a pre-trial order, the court may permit withdrawal or amendment when the presentation of the merits of the action will be subserved thereby and the party who obtained the admission fails to satisfy the court that withdrawal or amendment will prejudice him in maintaining his action or defense on the merits. Any admission made by a party under this Rule is for the purpose of the pending action only and is not an admission by him for any other purpose nor may it be used against him in any other proceeding.

The request for admission rule is the area where your personal knowledge of all the facts in your case can give you some real upsmanship. On each of the good points in your case and each of the weak points in the other party's case, hammer away at request for admissions of facts. If you don't get the right responses--what you want--pepper him with additional written interrogatories and make him explain his lies. If you don't get what you want file a series of motions and seek orders from the judge requiring him to answer "in accordance with the spirit of the rules." Of course, this may take some time. But who's in a hurry? And if you press your adversary to making statements under oath that you can conclusively prove are false--take it to the DA and put him in jail!

Each time you prove a "fact" which the adverse party refused to admit on your request for admission of facts you should file a motion under Rule 37 to collect your costs, expenses and attorney fees. Now, this may take some time too. If his answers to written interrogatories are evasive or incomplete-- just file your motions. Be tough!

Rule 37 (c) is as follows:

(c) Expenses on Failure to Admit. If a party fails to admit the genuineness of any documents or the truth of any matters as requested under Rule 36, and if the party requesting the admissions thereafter proves the genuineness of the document or the truth of the matter, he may apply to the court for an order requiring the other party to pay him the reasonable expenses incurred in making that proof, including reasonable attorney's fees. The court shall make the order unless it finds that: (1) The request was held objectionable pursuant to Rule 36 (a); or (2) the admission sought was of no substantial importance; or (3) the party failing to admit had reasonable ground to believe that he might prevail on the matter; or (4) there was other good reason for the failure to admit.

This is really a very important tool in your discovery work. You may not collect a lot of "attorney's fees" but you sure can wear the other parties and their lawyers to a state of exhaustion.

If the adversary fails to answer written interrogatories or respond to any rule you may haul him down to the judge and get an order directing him to comply-- and in some cases you may get a court order providing:

(1) That the matters regarding which the order
     was made or any other designated facts shall
     be taken to be established for the purposes
     of the action in accordance with the claim
     of the party obtaining the order;

(2) An order refusing to allow the disobedient
     party to support or oppose designated claims
     or defenses, or prohibiting him from intro-
     ducing designated matters in evidence;

(3) An order striking out pleadings or parts
     thereof, or staying further proceedings
     until the order is obeyed, or dismissing
     the action or proceeding or any part thereof,
     or rendering a judgment by default against
     the disobedient party; and

(4) In lieu of any of the foregoing orders or
     in addition thereto, an order treating as
     a contempt of court the failure to obey
     any orders except an order to submit to a
     physical or mental examination.

In lieu of any of the foregoing orders or in
addition thereto, the court shall require the party
failing to obey the order, or the attorney advising
him or both, to pay the reasonable expenses, including
attorney's fees, caused by the failure, unless the
court finds that the failure was substantially justified or that other circumstances make an award of
expenses unjust. You can have a lot of fun with this
rule if you follow all the procedures.

7. Suggested Discovery Strategy

Now that you have reviewed the discovery rules,
here's a few suggestions about how you can proceed

to (1) whip saw an adversary to the point where he will wish he had never thought of getting into a lawsuit with you, (2) discover enough evidence and defenses to win the case one way or another—either on procedural grounds or at trial, or (3) collect enough facts, records, documents, data, exhibits and other evidence to make a lengthy trial very distasteful to the other parties and their attorneys. In some courts—in some cases—justice doesn't always go to the kind at heart! You have to look out for yourself—nobody else will!

As soon as you get the case ready to go to court you should go to the closest library and spend a day or two. Look up all the general law—and statutory law of your state on the legal issue involved in your case. Contracts, bills and notes, debts, open accounts, guaranty, consumer contracts, breach of contract, loans, interest, usury, warranty, etc. Second, get your own copy of the general court rules and any local court rules. Study the rules carefully, find the clerk's office, ask the clerk about filing fees, court forms, the number and names of all the judges (especially the judge assigned to your case), the name and address of the official court reporter, and any other information the clerk, bailiff, secretary, or judge will discuss with you. Ask the clerk all about court procedures, files, forms, calendars, appointments, hearings, etc. But--do not ask him for legal advice: he will be embarrassed, he is not allowed to give it--you may be embarrassed--and that's not where you want to get your legal information. Go to the library for that. Listen to all he has to say about court procedures. Specifically ask the clerk what procedures are followed for getting a hearing on motions--get a copy of local court rules that tell you all about this--and be sure you understand the "hearing" procedures.

You should be able to get all this done in a few days after you get your own facts and evidence assembled.

8. Your Strategy As A Plaintiff

As a plaintiff your main strategy is to make sure you know all the facts and evidence necessary to prove your case, and, second, getting that evidence ready for admission in court. Frequently you can use the Request For Admissions rule to make the defendant admit most of the essential elements of your case. For example, if you sue on a $1000 note you can make him admit he signed the note, that the document is genuine, that your check to him for $1000 was the consideration for the note, and that he has not repaid it. In this case you'd be entitled to win if he admits all this--unless he has some affirmative defenses.

9.   Your Strategy As A Defendant

First, from your study of the complaint, your research of the law and your review of the affirmative defenses in the court rules, write down--in draft form-- your answer to the complaint. Analyze the facts you have available and list two--three--four--of your best points. Offense and Defense. Concentrate on these points throughout the litigation. List all other possible points in your case--offense and defense-- as a secondary battlefield.

Second, list in writing the two--three-four weakest points in the plaintiff's case. Don't worry too much at this point about the evidence--that comes later-- much later--just list all the points in plaintiff's case that a typical juror might not like. Put them down in writing with your answer and the Points And Defenses In Your Case.

Third, here are a series of things you should consider:

a.   Propound your first set of written interrogatories

to the plaintiff, as many as you need, directed mainly at getting names and addresses of witnesses, identification "sufficient for identification and description in a motion to produce" of documents, records, exhibits and other "relevant" things in the case. There are several sets of books in the law libraries that give examples of the kind of questions for written interrogatories that pull the best answers.

b. File your first set of Request For Admission of Facts in which you request the plaintiff to admit all the good, factual points in your case. Especially the ones you know you can prove. Don't list controverted, vague, uncertain points--or points you know he will deny--use only those crisp, specific facts you know an honest plaintiff would have to admit under oath. You may throw in one or two vague one's so you can later go to court on a hearing to compel a more direct answer. This may delay the case--but you can get a lot of information this way.

Keep in mind that this first set of written interrogatories is directed mainly at identifying where facts, information and evidence is located and who has it--you'll get to that later.

c. Along with the Request For Admission of Facts consider (optional) filing a second set of written

interrogatories in which you track your Requests on
the major points in your case and the major weaknesses
of plaintiff's case--and on each point propound the
following interrogatory: "If you deny Request For
Admission 3, 4, etc. . filed simultaneously herewith,
explain specifically, with particularity, and in
detail each and every fact, piece of evidence and
reason why you make such denial under oath." Do this
only for the big ones--your good points you know you
can prove if you have to.

Fourth, consider your Rule 12 Motions. These
have already been discussed in general, but you need
to give them careful thought after you have prepared
some of the other items. But remember that most of
the Rule 12 Motions must be filed before you file an
answer.

Study rule 12 (or your comparable court rule)
carefully and look at the annotations of the court
cases that construe the rules. You must be familar
with the local cases construing your rules. A few
hours in the law library will give you a good idea
of how to handle the motions. Write down the citations
to some of the cases--and when time permits--read them.

Consider a Motion To Dismiss (or demurrer) based
on each of the points listed in Rule 12. Those that

hold water--use them--file your motions, and be careful to file an affidavit--or other evidence--where
needed to support your points.

Consider a Motion For More Definite Statement
(or Bill of Particulars) on any points in the complaint that are vague or ambiguous.

Consider a Motion To Strike any "redundant,
immaterial, impertinent, or scandalous matter" in the
complaint. Use this motion carefully--and cautiously.
Read the local cases before using it.

Be sure to check your local court rules to determine whether a brief or memorandum of authorities
is required when you file your motions. In some
courts, especially the busy, over crowded ones, the
local rules provide that in some motions the parties
have to file briefs, and the judge may rule on the
motions without a hearing. If you fail to file a
brief when they are required, usually filed with the
motion--or within 10 days, the judge usually denies
your motion without looking at it--and without giving
it a fleeting thought. But look at it from the judge's
point of view; he has many cases, is very busy, sometimes overworked, and some lawyers file tons of paper
just for delay or from habit. The judges require the
briefs to discourage the filing of so many motions.

You don't have to write a legal treatise; the judge knows more about the rules and cases than you or most lawyers, but your job is to help him by writing down on paper the authorities he already knows about. Moreover, the judge thinks that if you and the lawyers have to look up cases to cite in the briefs you may learn something about the issues raised in the motions. It is a convenience for the judge, and typically it need be no more than a page or two. Sometimes only a citation to a court rule, or to one or two cases on your specific point will do it.

File your counterclaims, cross-claims, and third party complaints where the facts justify it. Do not file any sham or frivolous pleadings, but if you have a good cause of action, or probably have one, go at it full speed. Don't hesitate to be a detective and do some investigating yourself to get facts and evidence to support your case. If a witness is reluctant to talk to you explain in detail to him the rules of court on depositions. Ask him if he wants an official subpoena, an official hearing, under oath, before an official court reporter who takes down every word he says. And don't just make empty threats--be prepared to carry through with it if necessary.

The third party practice can be a little tricky
so study the rule carefully and try to file it before
you file your answer so you won't have to get special
permission from the judge.

Remember, don't file your answer until all the
Rule 12 Motions have been ruled on by the judge.
Sometimes one of these motions can get lost in the
shuffle of papers and as long as the judge hasn't
ruled on it you don't have to file an answer.

After you get answers to the first set of written
interrogatories, set down and carefully propound a
second set of interrogatories in which you ask specific,
particular, exact questions about all the documents,
records, evidence and witnesses the parties told you
about in the answers to your first set of written
interrogatories. If the other party doesn't answer
the interrogatories to your satisfaction you simply
file a set of motions and tell the judge about it!
File another set of Request For Admissions of Facts,
if appropriate.

Where you are a defendant and the plaintiff makes
objections to any of your written interrogatories or
Request For Admissions of Facts just let them set
there--forever if possible. Don't you call his
objections up for hearing yet. Even though some

rules require a party to set his own objections for hearing, the lawyers are frequently too busy to do it, or they overlook it. If the plaintiff ever proceeds further in the case you can move for a continuance or call up for hearing his objections to your written interrogatories and file a Motion To Compel Plaintiff to Answer the Written Interrogatories. You see, this is all in accordance with the rules. Generally the plaintiff can't get his case set for trial until the pleadings are settled, and motions disposed of. Don't hurry. The pleadings are not settled as long as motions are pending and undisposed of.

After all the Rule 12 Motions have been ruled upon by the judge--file your answer. Set up all defenses available to you which you can support by evidence and get ready to prepare for trial.

Proceed with further discovery if and when appropriate.

Wait a while and if your adversary ever wants to talk about settlement you might want to think about it. But don't hurry.

You might be having so much fun you won't want to settle.

J.   Devices For Terminating Litigation Without
     Trial

The Summary Judgment Rule is a big gun; here it is.

Rule 56.   Summary Judgment
(a)   For Claimant. A party seeking to recover
upon a claim, counterclaim, or corss-claim or
to obtain a declaratory judgment may, at any
time after the expiration of 20 days from the
commencement of the action or after service of
a motion for summary judgment by the adverse
party, move with or without supporting affidavits
for a summary judgment in his favor upon all or
any part thereof.

(b) For Defending Party. A party against whom
a claim, counterclaim, or cross-claim is asserted
or a declaratory judgment is sought may, at any
time, move with or without supporting affidavits
for a summary judgment in his favor as to all
or any part thereof.

(c) Motion and Proceedings Thereon. The motion
shall be served at least 10 days before the time
fixed for the hearing. The adverse party prior
to the day of hearing may serve opposing affidavits.
The judgment sought shall be rendered forthwith
if the pleadings, depositions, answers to interrogatories, and admissions on file, togehter with
the affidavits, if any, show that there is no
genuine issue as to any material fact and that
the moving party is entitled to a judgment as
a matter of law. A summary judgment, interlocu-
tory in character, may be rendered on the issue
of liability alone although there is a genuine
issue as to the amount of damages.

(d) Case Not Fully Adjudicated on Motion. If
on motion under this rule judgment is not rendered upon the whole case or for all the relief
asked and a tril is necessary, the court at the
hearing of the motion, by examining the pleadings
and the evidence before it and by interrogating
counsel, shall if practicable ascertain what
material facts exist without substantial controversy and what material facts are actually and
in good faith controverted. It shall thereupon
make an order specifying the facts that appear

without substantial controversy, including the
extent to which the amount of damages or other
relief is not in controversy, and directing
such further proceedings in the action as are
just. Upon the trial of the action the facts
so specified shall be deemed established, and
the trial shall be conducted accordingly.

(e) Form of Affidavits; Further Testimony;
Defense Required. Supporting and opposing
affidavits shall be made on personal knowledge,
shall set forth such facts as would be admissible
in evidence, and shall show affirmatively that
the affiant is competent to testify to the
matters stated therein. Sworn or certified
copies of all papers or parts thereof referred
to in an affidavit shall be attached thereto
or served therewith. The court may permit
affidavits to be supplemented or opposed by
depositions, answers to interrogatories, or
further affidavits. When a motion for summary
judgment is made and supported as provided in
this rule, an adverse party may not rest upon
the mere allegations or denials of his pleading, but his response, by affidavits or as otherwise provided in this rule, must set forth
specific facts showing that there is a genuine
issue for trial. If he does not so respond,
summary judgment, if appropriate, shall be
entered against him.

(f) When Affidavits Are Unavailable. Should
it appear from the affidavits of a party opposing
the motion that he cannot for reasons stated
present by affidavit facts essential to justify
his opposition, the court may refuse the application for judgment or may order a continuance
to permit affidavits to be obtained or depositions
to be taken or discovery to be had or may make
such other order as is just.

(g) Affidavits Made in Bad Faith. Should it
appear to the satisfaction of the court at any
time that any of the affidavits presented pursuant to this rule are presented in bad faith
or solely for the purpose of delay, the court
shall forthwith order the party employing them
to pay to the other party the amount of the
reasonable expenses which the filing of the
affidavits caused him to incur, including reasonable attorney's fees, and any offending party
or attorney may be adjudged guilty of contempt.

Summary Judgment is the procedure by which cases coming within its scope may be disposed of quickly, without delay and without the necessity of trial when the facts show that there is in fact nothing to be tried.

The purpose of the summary judgment rule is to avoid the time, labor and expense to counsel, parties, court and jury involved in an unnecessary trial. If it appears at the hearing of the motion for summary that there actually is not substantial controversy as to any material fact and that the movant is entitled to a judgment as a matter of law, the advantages of early recognition of that situation are obvious.

This motion is my favorite. It attacks the "merits" of the case, and is designed to pierce the pleadings to show that the other party's case has no merits based on the evidence, regardless of what is alleged in the pleadings. The old difference between the allegata and the probata.

The basis for the motion is that looking at all the evidence there is no genuine issue as to any material fact, and that you are entitled to a jdugment as a matter of law. This is usually filed after discovery proceedings and is normally based upon admissions made in pleadings, depositions, testimony, answers to written interrogatories, answers to request for admission

of facts, or matters of which judicial notice may be
taken by the court.

But one of the most common sources of evidence--
the easiest and most frequently used for this purpose
is an affidavit. Your affidavit must be based on personal knowledge (not hearsay), and must show that the
person giving the affidavit or statement is competent
to testify as to the matters stated in the affidavit.
Usually you can file this motion at any time--even with
your answer in the proper case. Or if you are the
plaintiff you can file it as soon as the defendant
files his answer.

Generally, if the affidavits or other evidence
filed with the court raise no genuine triable issue
of fact, then the court must enter summary judgment
for the moving party. Indeed, there would be nothing
to do at trial. You ought to read the annotations
under this rule to get a good idea of the kind of
cases the judges will give summary judgment on. Here
is an example:

Suppose you got sued by John Doe for $50,000 on
a $30,000 gambling debt and a $20,000 loan he made you
12 years ago. Assume gambling is illegal in your state
and that the statute of limitations on a loan in your
state is 10 years. You could file your answer under

admitting the gambling debt, and admitting the "loan,"
but allege that gambling is illegal in your state and
that the 10 year statute of limitation had run on the
loan. You file a Motion For Summary Judgment. You
Win! No trial. Same result with most of the affirmative defenses.

Note that Rule 56 (d) (and most state court rules)
provides that the court at the hearing of the motion,
by examining the pleadings and the evidence before it
and by interrogating counsel, shall, if practicable,
ascertain what material facts exist without substantial
controversy and what material facts are actually and
in good faith controverted. It shall thereupon make
an order specifying the facts that appear without
substantial controversy, including the extent to which
the damages or other relief is not in controversy, and
directing such further proceedings in the action as
are just.

This procedure is almost like a pre-trial conference, but you can sneak up on a lot of lawyers--the
overworked, inexperienced, lazy, sloppy ones and gain
many advantages with this maneuver. It works great with
a verified answer. See the Long Form Motion For Summary
Judgment. Lawyers won't be expecting this kind of ploy
fron a non lawyer.

If you are the defendant there are several other procedures to terminate a lawsuit in your favor without going to trial. Here are some of them.

(1) Voluntary Dismissal by Plaintiff

This happens more often than you think--especially when a plaintiff pays his lawyer $1000 or more in fees on a $500 case he hasn't got to trial yet! Given enought time he will soon recognize the economic realities of paying lawyer fees. If you hammer away at discovery enough many lawsuits are forgotten. And paying a lawyer "for noting" will get the plaintiff's attention fast.

(2) Involuntary Dismissal

This may happen where a plaintiff fails to obey an order of court--like an order to answer written interrogatories. The court simply dismisses his case if he doesn't comply with an order, or if he fails to comply with statutory requirements or court rules. If you press enough on discovery and motions you can't miss! You see, each time you hit them with pleadings or discovery it costs your adversary $50 to $80 per hour for his lawyer to respond.

(3) Lack of Prosecution

You can win many cases this way. Most courts have a rule that if the plaintiff takes no steps to prosecute his case (usually for 1 year) by bringing the case to trial it may be dismissed. Where you wear the plaintiff and his lawyer out with pleadings and discovery for a few months they will frequently lose interest in pushing the case to trial. Just let it lay there. This is likely to happen where a plaintiff gets tired pouring money into the lawyer's bank account, but has too much pride to take a voluntary dismissal--he won't mind letting the case die a natural death. And the lawyer won't care either. You'd be surprised to know the number of violent fights I've seen between plaintiffs and their own lawyers. You can generate this kind of situation if you keep the pressure on. Most courts are so crowded it literally takes years to get a case on the trial docket.

(4) Motion For Judgment On the Pleadings

This Rule 12 Motion is not much: it is similar to a motion to dismiss (demurrer) and is based on the proposition that the pleadings are insufficient as a matter of law to establish a claim or defense. You can try it anyway if you have good grounds.

K. Pre-Trial Conference

Rule 16. Pre-Trial Procedure; Formulating Issues
In any action, the court may in its discretion
direct the attorneys for the parties to appear
before it for a conference to consider

(1) The simplification of the issues;
(2) The necessity or desirability of amend-
    ments to the pleadings;
(3) The possibility of obtaining admissions
    of fact and of documents which will
    avoid unnecessary proof;
(4) The limitation of the number of expert
    witnesses;
(5) The advisability of a preliminary refer-
    ence of issues to a master for findings
    to be used as evidence when the trial is
    to be by jury;
(6) Such other matters as may aid in the dis-
    position of the action.

The court shall make an order which recites the
action taken at the conference, the amendments
allowed to the pleadings, and the agreements
make by the parties as to any of the matters
considered, and which limits the issues for trial
to those not disposed of by admissions or agreements of counsel; and such order when entered
controls the subsequent course of the action,
unless modified at the trial to prevent manifest
injustice. The court in its discretion may
establish by rule a pre-trial calendar on which
actions may be placed for consideration as above
provided and may either confine the calendar to
jury actions or to non-jury actions or extend
it to all actions.

Some courts require a pre-trial conference, some
make it discretionary with the judge; some do neither.
Check your local rules and customs. Generally this
is influenced by the attitude of the local judges and
this is one of the "local" rules, practices and customs
you need to ask the clerk about. Most judges use the
rule to some extent.

Where the pre-trial conference is held, it is
usually informal, usually in the judges chambers, and
only attorneys or parties attend. No witnesses or

evidence is presented. Most judges first explore the settlement possibilities and then follow their own version of the schedule in Rule 16. Some judges prepare the pre-trial order--most do not; some ask one' of the lawyers to prepare the order. If the judge asks the other lawyer to prepare an order make sure you ask the judge to let you help; don't trust the lawyer on the other side. He will give you the shaft every chance he gets--and he will usually be sanctimonous about it. Sometimes you can convince the judge at the pre-trial conference that you are entitled to a summary judgment, and he has the power to grant it at the pre-trial conference even if you have not filed a formal motion for summary judgment.

The following forms are the pleading and discovery tools you can use to "win" your cases; if you use them effectively you will be a consistent winner.

Form 12:   Answer

IN THE DISTRICT COURT IN AND

FOR ANYWHERE COUNTY

STATE OF ANYWHERE

Civil Action No____

JOHN DOE,   )

    Plaintiff   )

    v.   )   ANSWER

RICHARD ROE,   )

    Defendant   )

Defendant answers the complaint as follows:

1.   Defendant denies the allegations of paragraph 1.

2.   Defendant admits the allegations of paragraph 2.

3.   Defendant admits he signed a promissory note as alleged in the complaint but denies that he owes the plaintiff any sum whatsoever as is more specifically alleged hereafter.

4.   Defendant is without sufficient knowledge or information to form a belief of the allegations of paragraph 4 of the complaint and therefore denies the same.

FIRST DEFENSE

5.   The complaint fails to state a claim upon which relief may be granted.

Form 12:   Answer   (continued)

SECOND DEFENSE   (Statute of Frauds)

6.   The purported contract set forth in plaintiff's complaint by which defendant is sought to be charged is not in writing and signed by defendant or by some person authorized by defendant, as required by_____ (cite statute).   Furthermore, there is no note or memorandum of the alleged contract subscribed by defendant or by his agent, as required by said statute.

THIRD DEFENSE   (Accord and Satisfaction)

7.   On or about July 4, 1978, an agreement was reached between defendant and plaintiff that in satisfaction of any and all claims that plaintiff might have against defendant at the date thereof defendant should pay to the plaintiff the sum of $500 in full satisfaction of any and all claims of plaintiff against defendant as aforesaid, even though defendant at the time of making the said agreement and payment disputed and denied the claim of plaintiff, it being defendant's contention that the claims had been paid in full.   Therefore, defendant does not owe plaintiff any money whatsoever.

FOURTH DEFENSE   (Duress)

8.   The instrument sued on herein was obtained from defendant by plaintiff by duress of defendant sufficient

to deny defendant the exercise of his free will, when plaintiff, on the 28th day of June, 1977, at City, State, threatened defendant with_____(state the specific threats) under the following circumstances:__. Defendant, fearful and apprehensive of the possible consequences of the act threatened by plaintiff, executed and delivered the instrument solely as a result of plaintiff's threats, and for no other reason.

FIFTH DEFENSE   (Statute of Limitations)

9. This action was not commenced within____years after the cause of action accrued, consequently, it is barred by the applicable statute of limitation of this state (cite statute).

Wherefore, defendant having fully answered the complaint demands that the same be dismissed and defendant be awarded his cost, expenses and attorneys fees.

I hereby certify that a copy hereof was mailed to Black Jack, attorney for plaitiff, 123 Thirteenth Street, City, State, 12345, this ____day of May, 1978.

Richard Roe
88 Christmas Tree Drive
Nacogdoches, Texas 98889
707-888-8888
In Pro Per

Form 13: Counterclaim (See Form 12 for Caption)

Defendant, Counterclaimant, sues the plaintiff, counterdefendant and alleges:

1. That on the 1st day of June, 1978, counterclaimant bargained with counterdefendant for the purchase of a horse belonging to counterdefendant and that the counterdefendant, to induce counterclaimant to buy the horse and to pay the sum of $1000 therefor, represented to counterclaimant that the horse was sound in wind and limb, and free from any defect whatsoever.

2. That counterclaimant, believing defendant's statements to be true, and induced thereby, bought the horse paying the counterdefendant the sum of $1000 by the execution of a promissory note dated July 1, 1978.

3. That counterdefendant made the aforesaid representations knowing them to be false and with the intent to induce counterclaimant to make the purchase and to defraud him.

4. That the horse was in fact unsound, being then, and for a long time prior to the sale, inflicted with an incurable disease called cyphalothrixrhusio-pathia.

5. That counterclaimant has expended the sum of $3000 in feeding and taking care of the horse and in endeavoring to cure him of the disease, and has been put to other expenses, embarrassment and humiliation.

Form 13: Counterclaim (Continued)

Wherefore counterclaimant demands judgment against the counterdefendant for the sum of $5000 plus interest, court costs, expenses, attorneys fees and for such other and further relief as to the court seems just and proper.

(Certificate of Service)   (Signature)

Form 14: Cross-Claim (See Form 12 for Caption)

Defendant, cross-claimant, sues the co-defendant _____, and alleges:

1. (similar allegations as complaint or counter-claim).

(Certificate of Service)   (Signature)

Form 15: Third Party Complaint (See Form 12 for Caption)

Defendant, Third Party Plaintiff, sues_____, Third Party Defendant, and alleges:

1. Plaintiff, John Doe, has filed against defendant a complaint, copy of which is attached hereto as Exhibit C.

2. (Here state the grounds upon which you are entitled to recover from the thire party defendant, all or part of what the plaintiff may recover from you. The allegations should be framed similar to those in the complaint and the counterclaim).

Form 15:   Third Party Complaint (Continued)

Wherefore, Third Party Plaintiff demands judgment against the Third Party Defendant for all sums that may be adjudged against defendant in favor of plaintiff.

(Must be served on the third
 party with summons; and send
 copies to other parties)   (Signature)

Form 16:   Motion To Bring In Third Party Defendant
           (See Form 12 for Caption)

Defendant moves for leave to make_____a party to this action and that there be served upon him summons and third party complaint as set forth in Exhibit D, attached hereto.

(Certificate of Service)   (Signature)

Form 17:   Notice To Take Deposition (See Form 12 for
           Caption)

Notice is hereby given that defendant will take the deposition of plaintiff, John Doe, at 9 A.M. on Tuesday, July 20, 1978, at the offices of Richard Roe, 88 Christmas Tree Drive, Nacogdoches, Texas 98889, before_____, court reporter, or some other person authorized to take depositions in this state, said deposition to continue from day to day until completed.

(Certificate of Service)   (Signature)

Form 18: Written Interrogatories to Parties (See
          Form 12 for Caption)

Plaintiff is required to answer the following

interrogatories in accordance with the applicable

court rules:

1.   (Here ask any and all questions that are

relevant or that might lead to the discovery of

relevant evidence). See Bender's Forms of Discovery.

(Certificate of Service)   (Signature)

Form 19: Request For Admissions (See Form 12 for
          Caption)

Defendant requests that plaintiff, within_____

days after service of this request, make the following

admissions for the purpose of this action only and sub-

ject to all pertinent objections to admissability

which may be interposed at trial:

1.   That the documents described as Exhibits____

herein are genuine.

2.   That each of the following statements is true:

a.
b.
c.

3.   That the allegations contained in paragraph

3 of defendant's answer herein are true and correct.

4.   (Here list any other facts or issues) See
     Bender's Forms of Discovery.

(Certificate of Service)   (Signature)

Form 20: Motion For Order Requiring Plaintiff to Answer
          Written Interrogatories (See Form 12 for
          Caption)

Defendant moves for the entry of an order directing
the plaintiff to answer written interrogatories number
1, 5, 7, 8, 9, and 12 propounded on June 2, 1978, in
accordance with the rules of court.

(Certificate of Service)   (Signature)

Form 21: Motion For Summary Judgment--Short Form
          (See Form 12 for Caption)

Defendant moves for the entry of a summary judgment
in favor of the defendant and aginst the plaintiff on
the grounds that there are no genuine issues of any
material facts and defendant is entitled to a judgment
as a matter of law. This motion is based upon the
pleadings, affidavits, depositions, and answers to
written interrogatories filed in this cause including
affidavit attached hereto as Exhibit E.

(Certificate of Service)   (Signature)

Form 22: Motion For Summary Judgment--Long Form
          (See Form 12 for Caption)

Defendant moves for the entry of a summary judgment
in favor of the defendant and agsinst the plaintiff on
the grounds that there are no genuine issues of any
material fact and that defendant is entitled to a judgment as a matter of law. In the alternative, if judg-

ment is not rendered upon the whole case or for all
the relief asked and a trial is necessary, the Court
at the hearing of the motion, by examining the pleadings and evidence before it and by interrogating
counsel and the parties ascertain what material facts
exist without substantial controversy and what material
facts are actually and in good faith controverted, and
make an order specifying the facts that appear without
substantial controversy, and directing such further
procedings in the action as may be just and proper.

> Note: This kind of motion is generally not
> appropriate in personal injury cases or in
> cases which turn primarily on adjudication
> of fact questions, but is more generally
> applicable to situations in which there
> are, or may be, issues of law raised by
> the complaint and defenses which should
> be determined by the trial court prior
> to trial.

(Certificate of Service)   (Signature)

Form 23:   Final Summary Judgment (See Form 12 for
           Caption)

This cause came on for hearing on Defendant's
motion for summary judgment and the court having
reviewed the file, heard arguments of counsel and the
parties, and being fully advised in the premises finds
that there are no genuine issues of material fact and
that defendant is entitled to a judgment as a matter
of law, and it is therefore

Form 23: Final Summary Judgment (Continued)

ADJUDGED that the motion is hereby granted and judgment is hereby entered in favor of the defendant and against the plaintiff and the defendant shall have his costs upon appropriate application for which let execution issue.

Done and ordered this 15th day of June, 1978, at Miami, Florida.

_____
Judge

Form 24: Motion For Continuance (See Form 12 for Caption)

Defendant moves for a continuance of the trial in this action on the following grounds:

1. The cause for continuance arose after setting of the action for trial and is due to circumstances beyond defendant's control.

2. This action is one for_____. In order for defendant to establish his defense, it will be necessary to prove_____(set forth issues in case).

3. The only person having knowledge of these facts is _____, who is now at_____. He will testify as follows:_____(set forth the testimony).

4. Defendant has exercised due diligence to obtain the presence of the witness at trial. The following steps have been taken (list them).

Form 24: Motion For Continuance (Continued)

5. Despite defendant's acts, the witness will not be available because (give reasons), but defendant believes the witness will be available on_____because _____(set forth facts showing reasonable grounds to believe witness will be present at that time).

6. The procedure for taking of the witness's deposition in this case is not satisfactory because (give reasons).

(Certificate of Service)   (Signature)

Form 25: Order Granting Motion For Continuance
          (See Form 12 for Caption)

This cause was heard on defendant's motion for continuance of the trial and it is:

ADJUDGED AS FOLLOWS:

1. The Motion For Continuance is granted.

2. The action previously scheduled for trial on July 14, 1978, is reset for trial on August 14, 1978, at 9 A.M.

Done and ordered this 12th day of July, 1978 at Miami, Florida.

                              _____
                              Judge

Form 26: Final Judgment

IN THE DISTRICT COURT IN AND

FOR ANYWHERE COUNTY

STATE OF ANYWHERE

Civil Action No____

JOHN DOE,   )

    Plaintiff   )

    v.   )   FINAL JUDGMENT

RICHARD ROE,   )

    Defendant   )

This cause came on for jury trial on the 28th day of August, 1978, and the jury having returned a verdict in favor of the defendant it is

ADJUDGED as follows:

1. Final Judgment is hereby entered in favor of the defendant, Richard Roe, and against the plaintiff, John Doe, and the defendant shall go hence without day.

2. Defendant shall be entitled to costs on appropriate application for which let execution issue.

Done and Ordered this 31st day of August, 1978, at Denver, Colorado.

                             _____

                             Judge

CHAPTER IV

TRIAL

Here's where you can really have a lot of fun!

A trial is defined as the judicial investigation and determination of issues between the parties to an action. State statutes and court rules provide for the manner and procedures by which cases are placed on the trial calendar, and outlines the general order in which cases on the trial calendar will be disposed of. A great deal is left to the discretion of the trial judges.

The U.S. Constitution, Seventh Amendment, says, "In suits at common law, where the value in controversy shall exceed twenty dollars, the right of trial by the jury shall be preserved." Most states also have a similar constitutional provision.

However, your right to a jury trial is dependent upon timely demand. In the federal courts you must make a demand in writing and file it in court within 10 days after the filing of the last pleading (usually the answer) directed at any issue upon which the jury trial is sought. In the state courts there is usually a similar requirement; check your own court rules for the procedures.

In preparing for the trial you will need to do research on court procedures, watch some trials--as many as you can--and have your complete outline of everything you will present to the jury at trial. Write it all down--don't rely on your memory. Make sure you get all of your points, facts and evidence in the record. Your evidence is not good unless the jury hears it and your appeal record is not complete unless the court reporter gets it all down in writing. Double check to make sure you get all your defenses supported by evidence, where you have it. While this will be the most "fun" part of handling your own case, you will have to do some serious work and research in preparing your evidence and learning the basic proceedings in a jury trial even though the judge may give you help from time to time. Still, this is much better, far more fun, far more rewarding and productive, and far less expensive than paying a lawyer to do something you can do yourself.

A. Invoking The Rule

Before your trial starts you may, in most states, invoke the rule. This means that any party may ask the judge to order all witnesses in the case, except the parties, to stay out of the courtroom during the trial, and not talk to other witnesses, so they do

not hear other witnesses testify. The purpose of
excluding witnesses from the courtroom is to prevent
them from listening to testimony of the other witnesses and then shaping or fabricating testimony
accordingly. Generally this is a good idea--unless
you want your witnesses to hear the others testify.
If you wish to invoke the rule make sure you do it
before the trial begins.

B. Selection of The Jury

The easiest way to learn all about this proceeding
is to watch two or three or more jury trials in the
court--talk to lawyers--court bailiffs--court watchers--
court reporters--judges--and others who are familar
with court proceedings. You need to know the local
practice on jury challenges--the number of jurors--
their qualifications, what to ask on void dire (quali-
fication of jurors). Then go to the library and check
the statutes--rules--and cases--and the official Jury
Instructions for your court.

C. Opening Statement by Plaintiff

You can count on many lawyers to tell the jury
about his client's case--and then proceed to tell the
jury about what a bad guy the other party is. Don't
get in the gutter with him--take the high road--of
dignity--truth--honor. But if he gets out of bounds

you should object and move for a mistrial. Interrupt

opposing counsel in his opening and make a motion for

mistrial only if you know you have good grounds--or

that you can gracefully gain some good points with

the judge and jury. Opening statements are properly

for outlining to the jury the evidence to be presented--

not for argument of your case.

D. Opening Statement by Defendant

Be dignified, respectful, friendly, but not over

solicitious, to the judge and jury. Don't say bad

things--directly--about anybody. In your opening state-

ment to the jury (1) outline the good points of your

case in terms of facts and evidence that you plan to

present to them, and (2) describe for the jury the facts

and evidence about the other parties--but only the weak

points--not the strong points--ignore the good points

at this time. Remember you are an advocate--not an

objective observer--and you owe it to yourself to put

forth your side of the case. Essentially you want to

tell the jury about your case and in the process they

will learn a great deal about you.

E. Objections to Evidence; Motion To Strike
    Evidence; Motions For Mistrials

A party has the right to have his objections ruled

on, and if that right is not recognized by the trial

judge, with the result that improper evidence is

introduced to his prejudice, there is reversible error. Even if a judge asks a witness an improper question the party should object and insist on a ruling by the court.

In order to preserve the right to have a question reversed on appeal, a party must make his objection known at the earliest appropriate opportunity in order to give the trial judge the opportunity to take appropriate preventive or corrective action. In other words, you can't reverse a trial judge on appeal unless you give him a chance to rule the right way at the trial.

When objections are made reasons or grounds for the objections must be given. The old objection that the questions are irrelevant, immaterial and incompetent is the all-time favorite, but you don't usually get too far with it--unless you come up with a specific legal reason.

A motion to strike out evidence is the appropriate procedure where a witness is permitted to answer after objection to the question propounded to him, or where the witness, in response to a question which is relevant and proper, gives an incompetent answer. A motion to strike is proper where there has not been an opportunity to object previously because the question did not indicate the nature of the answer.

A motion for mistrial should be made where prejudicial evidence is introduced, or where opposing
counsel makes improper or prejudicial statements in
the presence of the jury. As a defendant you should
scream for a mistrial at every opportunity. The other
side may not be so anxious to have a retrial after he
pays his lawyer's fees.

F. Presentation of Evidence

Witnesses may testify to matters of fact. A
witness can tell what he saw, heard--except hearsay--
felt, smelled or touched through the use of his physical
senses. And a witness also may be used to identify documents, pictures or other physical exhibits to be put
in evidence at trial.

Generally, a witness cannot state his opinion or
give his conclusion unless he is an expert or especially
qualified to do so. In some instances, a witness may
be permitted to express an opinion, for example, as to
the speed an auto was traveling or whether a person was
intoxicated.

A witness who has been qualified in a particular
field as an expert may give his opinion based upon the
facts in evidence and may state the reasons for that
opinion. Sometimes the facts in evidence are put to

the expert in a question called a hypothetical question. The question assumes the truth of the facts contained in it. An expert witness may also state an opinion based on his personal knowledge of the facts through his own examination or investigation.

Generally, a witness cannot testify to hearsay, that is, what someone else has told him outside the presence of the parties to the action. Moreover, a witness is not permitted to testify about matters that are too remote to have any bearing on the decision of the case, or matters that are irrelevant or immaterial.

As a general rule you may not ask leading questions to your own witnesses, although it is a general custom to permit routine, noncontroversal information such as names, addresses, occupations, and the like to be elicited by leading questions. A leading question is one which suggests the answer desired.

You should make objections to leading questions, or to questions that call for an opinion or conclusion on the part of the witness, or require an answer based on hearsay. There are many other reasons for objections under the rules of evidence, and you should make a list of valid objections and a correct statement of reasons and legal grounds before the trial starts.

Objections are often made in the following form:

"Your Honor, I object to that question on the grounds that it is irrelevant and immaterial and for the further reason that it calls for an opinion and conclusion of the witness." Most courts require that the objection specify why the question is not proper. The judge will then rule on the objections. If the judge sustains an objection, another question should then be asked, or the same question be rephrased in proper form.

If an objection to one of your questions is sustained on either direct or cross-examination, you may make an offer to prove--or a proffer of evidence--as it is called. This offer is dictated to the court reporter away from the hearing of the jury. In your offer, you state the answer which the witness would have given if permitted to answer. The offer forms a part of the record if the case is later appealed.

When one party has finished his direct examination of a witness, the other party may then cross-examine the witness on any matter about which the witness has been questioned initially in direct examination. On cross-examination you may ask leading questions for the purpose of inducing a witness to testify about matters which he may otherwise have chosen to ignore or fail to mention.

On cross-examination, you may try to bring out

prejudice or bias of the witness, such as his relation-
ship or friendship to the party, or other interest in
the case. A witness can be asked if he has been convicted of a felony or crime involving moral turpitude,
since this bears upon his credibility.

After the opposing party has finished with his
cross-examination, the party who called the witness
has the right to ask questions on re-direct examination.
The re-direct examination covers new matters brought
out on cross-examination and generally is an effort to
rehibilitate a witness whose testimony on direct examination has been weakened by cross-examination.

In summary: Watch for "leading" questions and
hearsay. Make your objections when you know you are
right. Don't give the judge a "pain in the neck" by
making frivolous objections.

If you think one of the witnesses for the other
side is lying you can attack his credibility, but
make sure you have support for your position. You
can ask him: "Have you ever been convicted of perjury?"
"Do you have some special reason for not telling the
truth in this case?" Take your time to examine any
exhibits the other party offers in evidence. And
remember, you don't have to cross examine every witness.
Cross only if you can help your case.

Be sure you write down the questions before trial--
and know what the answers will be from all your wit-
nesses--and all opposing witnesses. When the other
party has testified, don't give him an opportunity to
repeat his best points--your chances of pulling a
Perry Mason are about Zero! That happens only on TV.
In other words he won't change his story. When a
witness lies once he will lie the second time much
easier. And he usually sticks to it 'til the bitter
end.

Don't let the attorney for the other side badger--
intimidate--or vilify your witnesses. Make objections
to the judge only. Don't argue or wrangle with the
opposing attorney--and don't make a speech to the jury
while making objections--always make your remarks to
the judge. Talking to the opposing lawyer in open
court is almost always bad--it is a loser--you can't
convince him of anything and you only give him help.
You work with the judge--stay on his side--and work
with the jury.

Some attorneys make snide remarks about the
adverse party--or their case--or their witnesses--and
while there is a wide discretion in what can be said
you should object to any personal attack, or matter
that is clearly improper, and, in the proper situation,
move for a mistrial.

G. Motion For Directed Verdict

When all the evidence is completed both parties generally ask the judge for a Directed Verdict. As a defendant, unless you are relying entirely on your affirmative defenses to win your case, you should always make a motion for a directed verdict at the close of the plaintiff's case, and again at the close of all the evidence. Check your rules and statutes and have all the "grounds" available for this motion and be sure you state them to the judge. You must state your grounds and reasons; have them written down in your outline.

H. Jury Argument

The plaintiff gets the open and close to the jury. You should develop the idea throughout the trial that you are the "good guy" and the other party and his attorney are vicious scoundrels. In your argument show the jury how you proved the points in your case that you told them about in the opening statement-- show them how the other party was weak--on the points you mentioned--and how you and the jury will work the whole thing out to make a final determination that will result in truth and justice. Avoid appeals to sympathy, passion and prejudice, the golden rule argument, race, religion, political, social, class or business prejudice,

pointing out wealth or poverty of litigants, appeal to
self interest of jurors as taxpayers, use of abusive
language, or attack on the other party or his attorney.
Stick with the facts--evidence--and the law. The
"golden rule" argument is telling the jury to place
themselves in the place of one of the parties. They
are supposed to be objective in their deliberations.

I. Burden of Proof; Jury Arguments

The plaintiff has the ultimate burden of persuasion as to the essential elements of his claims. The
defendant has the ultimate burden of persuasion on
his affirmative defenses raised in the pleadings.
Every court has a standard instruction on this point
and will always give it to the jury.

The burden of persuasion is to produce whatever
evidence is required to convince the trier of fact
(jury). In civil cases the judge will always instruct
the jury that this proof must be by a "preponderance"
of the evidence, as opposed to "beyond every reasonable
doubt" as required in criminal cases.

"Preponderance" of evidence is usually defined as
a situation where one side of the case is made to appear
more likely or probable to the trier of fact. It is
evidence that when weighed with that opposed to it, has
more convincing force, so that the probability of truth

lies therein. It is that evidence which is most convincing and satisfying in the controversy between the parties, regardless of which party may have produced the evidence.

As a defendant you can develop a mighty powerful argument to the jury about the mighty burden of proof the law imposes on the plaintiff. Use terms like "the plaintiff must prove all essential elements of his lawsuit by a preponderance of the evidence (emphasize the word Preponderance--as though it was the weight of the world)--by a "preponderating weight of all the credible evidence" (emphasize credible--and later tell them the plaintiff's evidence simply is not credible). Each argument you make on the good points of your case should end with the observation that "the burden of proof is on the plaintiff to prove his case by a preponderance of the evidence." That's a quick switch-- from your good points to plaintiff's burden--but true. Just don't bother to dwell on who has the burden to prove your defenses. In a close case this argument can make the difference. Keep in mind that most jurors don't know a lot about court procedures--you have a right and duty--as your own counsel--to tell them. And make them know it!

In your final summation to the jury consider a

wind-up something like this:

"And finally, Ladies and Gentlemen of the Jury . . ."

(1) Explain in high sounding phrases the high honor--duty--obligations--the jury has in maintaining truth and justice.

(2) Repeat the old "preponderance of the evidence" theme as to the entire case of plaintiff and every part of it--if you are the defendant.

(3) If you are the plaintiff emphasize the strong burden of proof the defendant has on his defenses.

(4) Summarize the good points of your case--and the weak points of the other party's case.

(5) End with a flag waving "we who labor here seek only the truth." Put your own personal touch and personality into it and let your imagination and emotions flow.

Before the case is submitted to the jury for a verdict, the trial judge will give the jury instructions to guide their deliberations. Typically, the instructions will specify the issues in dispute; which party has the burden of proof (persuasion) on each issue; the rules of substantive law applicable to each issue; the kinds of verdict the jury may return; the procedure to be followed in deliberation and reaching a verdict. Federal courts, and many state courts, permit the trial

judge to comment on the evidence to the jury. Most
judges do not.

The ultimate responsibility for instructing the
jury rests with the trial judge, and failure to provide
correct and complete instructions on every material
issue in a case is judicial error. But, in a practical
sense, counsel--or the party--owes a duty to the judge
to call to his attention any error in the instructions
which he proposes to give, to enable him to review and
correct the instructions before the matter is submitted
to the jury.

Generally, the trial judge must instruct the jury
on whatever theories of the case are reasonably supported
by the evidence regardless of whether he personally
believes that evidence. Each party has an absolute
right to have the jury instructed in accordance with
his version of the facts in the record. Make sure you
get the judge to cover all your points.

Practically all the state courts have an official
approved set of "Jury Instructions," usually approved
by the state Supreme Court. You can find this in most
law libraries--and in many public libraries and it is
very important for you to have this to get your proper
instructions to propose to the trial judge. Actually,
these instructions books are easy to use, but you have

to be careful not to overlook any theory of your case.
It is your responsibility and not necessarily the
judge's to find the law. Incidentally, these books
are an excellent short cut in your research. They
give citations to cases and authorities on each of
the legal issues covered.

In most civil trial courts the argument to the
jury comes before the judge gives the instructions to
the jury. The last words the jury hears are the judge's
instructions, rather than your brilliant argument.
Therefore, you must make a dynamic impression on the
jury so they will remember the important points in the
jury room. If you have good facts--the thrust of your
argument should be on the facts--if you don't have
good facts argue the law; if you don't have either--
smile.

If your facts and evidence are not especially great
on your side of the case talk about honesty, integrity,
charity, truth, justice, credibility of witnesses, fair-
ness, honor, fidelity, right, equity, trustworthiness,
freedom from fraud and chicanery, sincerity, candor,
innocence, plain-talk, clean hands, air tight case, fair
play, self-respect, square dealing, loyalty to principles,
impartiality of the jury . . . and that sort of thing.

Associate yourself and the jury with all of these
good qualities and with truth and justice.

Don't sling mud. Don't call names. Don't be rude to the other lawyer, the judge, jury or anybody else. You are Mr. Clean! Ignore the real damaging evidence of the other party unless you can explain it away--or destroy it.

Always have a written outline of your summation to the jury and be sure to cover all the points. Practice your "winding-up" part to make sure you can deliver it with conviction--emotions--and fire!

One of the ploys I always enjoyed was--in some cases--where there was one major issue of law that controls in the case, was to explain--very seriously that the judge will give the jury the law that controls in the case. But, tell them, your case is founded on one main issue. Explain that while it is the judge's statement of the law that counts you just want them to know that you are relying on one main issue of law in your case.

Then read verbatim from what you know the judge is going to tell them about your legal issue. Yell and scream to the jury that this is the "KEY" issue in the case--what the case is really all about. When the judge tells them your theory of the case--just as you told them--they will gain a new respect for you and your knowledge of the law. And maybe they will agree

with you. In all events the key point is to be honest
with the jury--but forceful.

The trial judge may, in his discretion, either
question any witness called by a party, or even call
and question witnesses of his own, but most judges
usually exercise this power sparingly, in order to
avoid claims of partisanship or prejudicing the jury.
And a few states even deny the right to trial judges
to call or ask questions of witnesses--on the ground
that the trial judge must act as an "umpire," not as
an advocate. Even so, when you represent yourself, if
you conduct yourself with dignity and a knowledge of
your case and your rights, the trial judge will usually
be very helpful in giving you some assistance in following the correct court procedures.

J.   Jury Verdict, Entry of Verdict and Entry of
     Judgment

After the verdict no matter who wins somebody has
to prepare a written judgment for the judge to sign
and "enter" in the court records to make it final.
Each court has its own practice but it is usually prepared by (1) the clerk, (2) the attorney of the party
who wins, (3) the judge (not likely), (4) the judge's
secretary, or (5) a combination of the above. If you
win be sure it is entered and you get a copy of it.
Don't trust a lawyer for the other side; watch him!

CHAPTER V

POST TRIAL MOTIONS AND MANEUVERS

You're not down yet. If the jury goes wrong--as they sometimes do--or if the judge makes a reversible error--you can handle it. There are several remedies you can employ to attack the trial court before resorting to an appeal.

A. Motion For Judgment Notwithstanding the Verdict
    (Non Obstento Veridicto)

A judgment N.O.V. nullifies the jury verdict; it is a judicial determination that regardless of the verdict, the evidence is legally insufficient to sustain the verdict and therefore you are entitled to a judgment in your favor. This is the same position you took when you filed your first pleading--don't back down from your position if you are right.

Generally the motion can be filed only (1) in jury trials, (2) if you made a motion for directed verdict at the close of plaintiff's case and/or at the close of all the evidence; and (3) if you make your motion timely (usually within 10 to 15 days after the verdict--or, in some courts, the entry of judgment.

B. Motion For New Trial

This is generally filed at the same time you file

your motion for judgment N.O.V. Typical of the grounds
on which a new trial may be granted in actions at law
are:

(1) Irregularities in proceedings, for example,
counsel's comment in argument to the jury on the poverty
of plaintiff and the wealth of defendant, false answer
by a juror on voir dire examination, etc.

(2) Misconduct of jury in deliberations or verdict.

(3) Accident or surprise, for example, some extra-
ordinary event that was prejudicial to you--against which
you exercised due diligence in seeking to protect yourself against, and where you sought relief (like a motion
for mistrial, request for continuance, etc) at the earliest possible opportunity.

(4) Insufficiency of the evidence.

(5) Newly discovered evidence that you--through
due diligence--could not have obtained before trial.

(6) Verdict or decision is against the law.

(7) Excessive or inadequate damages.

C. Motion To Vacate or Amend Judgment

This motion is directed to your steadfast efforts
to have the judge change the judgment to correct errors
of law--especially your argument that the evidence is
insufficient to sustain the verdict.

D. Motion For Relief From Judgment or Order

This motion is generally filed to correct clerical errors or mistakes, on grounds of inadvertance, surprise, excusable neglect of party or counsel, newly discovered evidence which by due diligence could not have been discovered in time to move for a new trial or fraud, misrepresentation or other misconduct by the other party, that the judgment is void as a matter of law, that it has been satisfied, or that a prior judgment upon which it is based has been reversed, or any other reason justifying relief from the operation of the judgment.

E. Independent Suit to Set Aside Judgment

The grounds for this kind of action are:

(1) Jurisdictional defects (lack of subject matter jurisdiction or lack of personal jurisdiction).

(2) Extrensic fraud or mistake.

F. Appeal

If you have come this far you can handle your own appeal, but we are counting on you to win most of your lawsuits in the trial courts.

CHAPTER VI

SMALL CLAIMS COURTS

A. Development of the Small Claims Courts
   in This Country

The development of small claims courts in the
United States is the result of reformist activity at
the beginning of this century. The reformers, among
them some of the most outstanding legal scholars of
their day, were particularly interested in relieving
the legal and monetary difficulties experienced by
the less effluent litigants and the individuals with
a valid but small monetary claim. In some states
these people could turn to the justice of the peace
courts, but these tribunals were confined to certain
areas and were notorious for the low quality of justice
they provided. Thus, no legal institution existed to
deal adequately with small claims at that time.

One of the early advocates of the small claims
courts was Dean Roscoe Pound who said:

> It is here that the administration of justice
> touches immediately the greatest number of people.
> It is here that the great mass of an urban popu-
> lation, whose experience of the law in the past
> has been too often experience only of the arbi-
> trary discretion of police officers, might be
> made to feel that the law is a living force for
> securing their individual as well as their col-
> lective interests. For there is a strong social

interest in the moral and social life of the individual. If the will of the individual is subjected arbitrarily to the will of others because the means of protection are too cumbrous and expensive to be available for one of his means or the inclination to resist, there is an injury to society at large. Pound, The Administration of Justice in the Modern City, 26 Harvard Law Review 302 (1913).

The general purpose of small claims courts is to provide a summary procedure, for the litigation of small claims, that is, claims not exceeding a certain specified amount--usually $500 to $1000. Therefore, certain legal technicalities that may encumber an ordinary proceeding are generally dispensed with in a small claims proceeding. However, the substantive law applicable in a small claims proceeding is the same as that applicable in a regular proceeding.

Typical of the court rules in small claims courts is that of New York which provides:

The court shall conduct hearings upon small claims in such manner as to do substantial justice between the parties according to the rules of substantive law and shall not be bound by statutory provisions or rules of practice, procedure, pleading or evidence." New York Civil Court Act Article 18, Section 1804 (McKinney Supp. 1972).

This is, of course, a perfectly reasonable provision, as cases involving very complicated substantive laws or rules can and should be removed by the judge to the regular civil courts.

The formal rules of evidence should not apply to

small claims procedures. The report of the National

Institute for Consumer Justice states that a court

attempting to force adherance by all small claims

litigants to the rules of evidence would have no time

to devote to the substance of the cases before it.

Because of the relative informality of most consumer

transactions, the majority of the consumers do not

receive or retain the evidence necessary to conform to

the formal rules of evidence. A Philadelphia small

claims court rule--in response to this reality provides:

> When a claim is based upon a written contract,
> three copies of at least pertinent portions must
> be filed with the statement of claim. However,
> if the contract is not available, it is sufficient
> simply to explain why and describe its provisions.
> Philadelphia Municipal Court Civil Procedure
> Rule 107 (e) (1971).

Another difficulty faced by many consumer plaintiffs

in recent years has been discovering the official legal

name of the firm they wish to sue. This often involves

intensive research into the files at municipal or state

offices. The problem should be resolved by allowing

suits to be brought in the name of the defendant listed

on their business premises, letterheads, or in advertise-

ments. Many courts have already implemented this practice.

B. Practice In Small Claims Courts

You need not retain a lawyer to sue in small claims

court. In fact, some courts don't permit attorneys.

Court filing fees usually range from $2 to $15, and judgment in your favor as a rule includes recovery of filing fees. You may state your grievance in plain words; you don't have to know a lot of legal jargon. In most small claims courts the judge won't insist on formal procedures or strict rules of evidence. You tell your side of the story and the other party tells his side. Cases come to trial as a rule without the long delays so common in most civil courts. Decisions are usually rendered immediately from the bench or within a few days after trial.

Almost every state has some kind of small claims court. The most you can claim is usually somewhere between $100 and $1000, but the trend is to higher limits. A few small claims courts handle cases up to $5000 or $10,000 or more. The defendant in some small claims courts can have a case transferred to civil court, where the proceedings are more formal. Either way you can handle it yourself.

Small claims courts are often called by other names, for example, justice court, district court, municipal court, justice of the peace, county court, civil court, magistrate's court, court of record, conciliation court, circuit court, court of common pleas, and others.

C.   How To Get A Case Started In Small Claims Court

Ask the court clerk whether the court can handle your kind of case. Get a copy of the court rules, if any. Most courts have jurisdiction over contractual disputes--the usual run of buyer-seller controversies involving money damages--and claims of damage through negligence, such as auto accident claims. Some large cities have special courts that handle landlord-tenant disputes.

You can also ask the clerk whether the court has jurisdiction over the party you wish to sue, but don't necessarily accept his word as final. The usual rule is that a defendant must live, work or do business in the court's territory. Complications may arise with out-of-town firms. You may have to file suit in the defendant's city or county instead of your own. This is the jurisdiction--venue problem. With an out-of-state firm, you may have to contact your state government (usually the secretary of state) to find out where to make service of process. If a firm does business in your state, they can be sued in your state. The clerk can help you in serving process. The success of your action may also hinge on whether the firm you sue is still in business and whether you can make the defendant pay a judgment. Don't waste a lot of time in litigation

unless you are fairly sure you will be able to collect
your judgment.

Double check the business name and address of the
company being sued. In some courts the suit may be
dismissed unless you have identified the company exactly
as it has registered itself for legal purposes. Ask
the clerk whether strict accuracy is required, and, if
so, how to find the correct name and address.

If you know a lawyer well enough to ask him a few
questions about small claims courts you can get some
good information--free. If you have the time you should
watch a session of the court in action before your own
case comes to trial.

Prepare for trial by gathering all pertinent receipts,
cancelled checks, contracts, bills, purchase orders,
written estimates, pictures and other documentary evidence.
It will help to set down the events in chronological order,
and check the dates carefully. Arrange for all witnesses
you may need to attend the trial and testify.

In disputes over workmanship, a disinterested person
in the same trade makes an ideal witness. If he won't
appear in person, his written statement may be viewed as
acceptable evidence in some courts--but not all. Check
with the clerk on this point. Bring to court the physical
evidence of your claim, such as clothing ruined by the

dry cleaner whom you are suing or a defective appliance, or any other exhibit or object you think will support your side of the case.

If your opponent offers to settle out of court, have him put it down in written form. A copy signed by both parties should be filed with the court so that the agreement can be enforced by law. Or you can ask him to appear with you in court to tell the judge the settlement terms and have it recorded by the judge. Always try to collect your court costs if possible. The court will usually award you the court costs if you win the case.

When you get to trial you merely state the facts of your case briefly and offer supporting evidence. Do not be overly contentious; refrain from making accusations about the defendant's behavior, motives or honesty. If you have a good case, the facts will make it for you. If you have trouble collecting after winning your case have the clerk issue a writ of execution or a writ of garnishment directed at the property and assets of the defendant. Help the sheriff find property belonging to the defendant.

The most important thing to do in getting ready for the trial is to know the date, time, and place of your trial and to be there on time. You should notify the clerk if you and the defendant settle your claim before the date set for trial.

If you are the defendant and you do not wish to contest the plaintiff's claim, you may settle with him before the date set for trial and have the action dismissed by the court. If you don't settle and do not appear at the trial, a judgment may be awarded by default against you. You may answer the complaint stating your defenses and you may also file a counterclaim against the plaintiff for any claims you may have against him. The clerk can explain the counterclaim procedures to you and usually provide appropriate forms to use.

Remember: Whether you are the plaintiff or the defendant, you have to appear at trial, or you may lose the case automatically. If there is some important reason why you can't be in court on the day of your trial, call the court clerk and try to arrange for a continuance of the trial to another date.

D. What To Do At Trial

The trial is just a simple, informal hearing before the judge or a referee. Try to get to court early so you will have time to find the small claims courtroom, but remember, there may be a number of cases to be heard so you will have to wait your turn. This will give you an opportunity to see how the court procedures work.

If the person you are suing does not appear for the trial, and he was properly served with the notice, then you will probably win your suit by default, but you may have to explain your case to the judge. If the defendant does appear, then the judge will hold a hearing and decide which of the parties should win the case. If you are the defendant and the plaintiff doesn't appear for the trial, the suit against you will usually be dismissed.

When your case is called, you should try to explain as simply as possible why the person you are suing owes you money. Be sure to offer all your evidence and witnesses. If you are the defendant, you will have an opportunity to explain why you don't owe the plaintiff the money he is suing you for. The judge may help both parties by asking questions, and you should try to answer these questions clearly and directly. There are usually a large number of small claims cases to be heard, and you have a limited time to present your case. Always have a written outline of all of your points and make sure they are all covered.

E. Getting Your Money After You Win

If the court decides in your favor a formal judgment
or court order will be entered. After you get the judgment you should make demand on the defendant to pay you
immediately. If he refuses to pay you the money after
you have received a judgment, you should then obtain
a writ of execution or garnishment from the court
clerk and have it served to seize any property or wages
of the defendant you can find. The court cannot collect
your money for you, so you have to be an investigator
to locate assets of the defendant yourself.

CHAPTER VII

HOW TO USE THE LAW LIBRARY
AND YOUR PUBLIC LIBRARY

You don't need any special legal training to do
the legal research needed to handle your own case in
accordance with the instructions in this book. You
will need time, interest, and perseverance--but that's
necessary for success in anything. Once you get into
it you will enjoy it.

As you know lawyers go to law school for three
years to learn "all the laws about everything" and to
learn how to research and find "all the laws." You
will have only the subject of your lawsuit to research;
your research is concentrated only on those legal issues
raised in your case--a case you know more about than
anybody else in the whole world. Your research is,
therefore, much easier and shorter, and not "all over
the ball park." Moreover, you will have a keen and
genuine personal interest in the legal issues in your
own case which makes it easier. Under these conditions
you will become an "expert" on the laws on your case
in a very short time. It is easier than you think.

There are several places where you can get the
information needed to handle your case. The following

are listed in order of preference in the number of
books available.

1. Law School Library

This is the place where you can find just about
everything available anywhere. There is one or more
in every state and you won't have any difficulty
locating one. Most are state supported schools and
the libraries are open to the general public. But,
a caveat: be sure you don't mark any books, damage them
in any way, and make sure you always follow all library
rules about the use of the books and library.

Librarians and law students are great helpers
in finding anything you want. Law students are
especially anxious to demonstrate how much they know
about legal research, and law books, and the law.
Strike up conversations with them (when they have the
time--and they can be very helpful. You should dress
appropriate for the atmosphere in a law library, do
not make noise or distract any other users of the
library--and other persons don't generally cause any
trouble for you. Once you get charged up about your
research, you'll really have a lot of fun.

Some large law school libraries (usually in large
metropolitan areas) charge a small fee for use of the
library. In this situation the law library is always

packed full of lawyers, professors, students, and other users anyway, therefore you are probably better off to go to the public library. Most public libraries in large cities have all the books you need.

You may want to look at several sources of law, but essentially the following sources are all you really need:

(1) Your state statutes and court rules;

(2) Digest of your state court decisions;

(3) Your court "Jury Instructions;" and

(4) Case Reports for your state.

2. University Library

Most of these libraries have a copy of your state statures, some have the case reports, and some have the Jury Instructions. These are generally public libraries and you should have no difficulty in finding what you need. Check the index first, and the librarian second!

3. Your State Supreme Court Library

If you live close to your state capital where your state Supreme Court is located, you're in luck. You can use these, but be sure you put on your best "dignity" and manners. Actually you don't find many supreme court judges there, but their law research clerks will be swarming all over the place. And here is where you may be in luck. If you can strike up a conversation with these guys you're really in luck; you got it made. They generally know all the laws, all the current decisions, all the court rules, and all about the trial judges. Don't ask them for legal advice, but ask them about general law issues--the issues you have in your case, and ask where to find the law. They know. They will be the most helpful people you will ever find. In a tough legal problem you might hire them--for a small fee--to do some research for you. They will do a better job than most any lawyer and charge less.

4. State Courthouse Law Library

This is the law library for the trial judges. Most are available for your use, and they almost always have everything the judges have available, therefore all you will need. Also, check to see if the trial judges have a law clerk. Some do; some don't. These research clerks are usually overworked, but they can also be very helpful in giving you tips about the trial judges, the court procedures, where to find the law you need, and just about anything else you need in a law library. Naturally, the librarian in all libraries is one of the best persons to consult. There's nothing wrong with you talking to the judges-- just don't talk to the judge on your case about your case.

5.   Public Library

Most general public libraries have the state
statutes, and some have the Jury Instructions and the
case reports. The librarians and research clerks in
these libraries are generally most helpful.

6.   Lawyer Office Library

Most lawyers have access to all the basic sources
listed above. Get friendly with some lawyer in the
larger firms in your town (they generally have more
books), possibly retain him for some simple legal
task (maybe writing a will). Most will be very co-
operative in letting you use their books if you take
good care of them and cooperate with his secretary.
In a large firm you will always find the youngest
lawyers burried in the law library. They are always
easy to talk to and they are also anxious to show off
about how smart they are. Ask them a few questions
and see how much free information you can get. In all
events you can have a handy library if you play it
right.

If your case is fairly complicated and involves
a substantial amount of money--go to one of the younger
lawyers in a big law firm. Talk to him about him representing you in your case. Don't make any committment--
talk to him about his fee arrangement--what tactics he
might take if he handles the case, etc. After he quotes

you a fee arrangement tell him you simply can't afford
a lawyer--"at this time"--but can you "use his library
to look up the law in your case" with the idea that
you _may_ be able to retain him (at his price) before
the trial. Don't make any definite committment--leave
it loose. In most circumstances he will be most
anxious to help you find the law, and he may visit
with you about your case during coffee breaks from
time to time! Who knows, you just may want to retain
him to help you try the case. At least its a darn
good option to have available. Besides, you need a
handy law library. Don't hesitate to ask.

Final word on libraries--and legal research. You
can learn more from judge's research clerks, law students
and other court personnel in a day than you can learn
pouring over law books for weeks. But you should do
both--just be efficient about it--take some short cuts.
Ask questions of everybody in sight--make notes--and
then go to the library to search out the law you have
learned about.

Generally you won't need to buy any books, except
that you should consider buying (or getting) a copy of
the Court Rules (about $5 to $15) and a copy of the local
court rules (frequently no cost or a nominal charge).

CHAPTER VIII

LAWYERS - JUDGES - COURTS - AND YOU

Who Is The Judge?

Lawyers and judges are human just like you and me.

But when people spend all that time going through college, law school (learning big words) and a few years of law practice they tend to form the idea that they are some kind of God.

When they get appointed or elected as a judge-- they are God!

Well, that story may not be all true, but it is one of the legends that many people believe to be true. The power that judges have is awesome. But judges have a constitutional duty to uphold the constitution and laws of the land--that is their full time job. They are human, and while human beings have flaws most of the judges try hard to do the right thing. But what is right for you--in your case--is your job. Judges make mistakes; it is your job to correct them if they happen to make a mistake in your case--by appeal. Don't be afraid of judges; and don't think you are imposing on them by taking their time to try your case--that's their job.

Your Attitude

In any contest (especially lawsuits) being aggressive
is one of the essential elements of success. And you
have to look like, act like, have the attitude of, and
be, a winner. The word "law" is defined as "rules of
civil conduct," or as I like to say, "the rules of
the game by which life is played." Certainly in a
court of law--where you are engaged in a lawsuit--a
contest--you have to play according to the rules laid
down in that forum (court). The judge is the referee
who can be reversed by a higher court. The Supreme
Court (of last resort)--right or wrong--has the final
word in this part of the game--the law. But what
happens in your case depends more on you and what you
do in preparation than on the other side, the judge
or the Supreme Court.

Preparation

Your attitude about lawyers, judges and court
personnel will play a big part in your success--or
lack of it. But let me give you the key word to describe your key to success--in lawsuits and in life:
PREPARATION!

In law school all my professors kept saying, "preparation for trial is the key to success as a lawyer.
Prepare." My reaction was, "Well, I know that; everybody knows that." Perhaps that's your thoughts. But

it didn't take me very long after starting law practice
to <u>understand</u> what was meant by preparation. It doesn't
matter whether you are by nature an aggressive person,
a quiet, easy going person, a big or little ego person,
or somewhere in between. If you prepare your case well,
you are a winner. If your lawsuit is important to you--
and it is--you will be motivated to work hard and get
"psyched up" about it. Spend all that excess energy
in digging, investigating, examining witnesses, finding
facts, getting exhibits, gathering evidence, doing your
research and all the items we have discussed about preparing your case for trial.

You and Your Case

Judges preside over hundreds of cases; lawyers
handle many cases. To them your case is just another
case on a docket sheet. But to you it is <u>your</u> case.
That's important. And its big. You know more about
it than anybody else, you can learn all about the
specific laws governing your case, and you can be in
charge of your case as it passes through the courthouse
on a long list of other cases. If you prepare it well,
all will end well.

Winners and Losers

In our society what is right, wrong, ethical,
moral, sinful, proper, illegal, dirty, unfair, lawful,
or inequitable is frequently a matter of opinion and
has many shades of grey. Ask Bert Lance. Or Richard
Nixon. When you, in your honest opinion, are right
you shouldn't let rain, sleet, snow or the dark of
night deter you in your quest for justice.

Tear 'em up Tiger!

GLOSSARY

Accord and Satisfaction. An agreement between two persons, one of whom has a right of action against the other, that the latter should do or give, and the former accept, something in satisfaction of the right of action different from, and usually less than, what might be legally enforced.

Action. A suit or process at law; the procedure of instituting a lawsuit in a court of law.

Adhesion Contract. A contract printed as a standard form, submitted by one party to the other on a take-it-or-leave-it basis. Adhesion contracts are commonly presented to consumers in situations where the buyer's position is substantially weaker than the seller's.

Affidavit. A written or printed declaration or statement of facts made voluntarily, and confirmed by the oath or affirmation of the party making it, taken before an officer having authority to administer oaths.

Affirmative Defenses. New matter constituting a defense; new matter which, assuming the complaint to be true, constitutes a defense to it.

Allegations. The assertion, declaration, or statement of a party to an action, made in a pleading, setting out what he expects to prove.

Allegata et probata. Latin. Things alleged and proved. The allegations made by a party to a suit, and the proof adduced in their support.

Annotations. A remark, note, or commentary on some passage of a book, intended to illustrate its meaning. Citations of cases construing statutes or other laws.

Answer. Strictly speaking, it is a pleading by which defendant in a suit at law endeavors to resist the plaintiff's demand by an allegation of facts, either denying allegations of plaintiff's complaint or confessing them and alleging new matter in avoidance, which defendant alleges should prevent recovery on facts alleged by plaintiff.

Arbitration. The submission for determination of dis-
   puted matter to private official persons selected
   in the manner provided by law or agreement.

Assumption of Risk. Exists where none of fault in injury
   rests with plaintiff, but where plaintiff assumes the
   consequences of injury occurring through fault of
   defendant, third person, or fault of no one. It is
   based upon the maxim "volenti non fit injuria," which
   means that to which a person assents is not regarded
   in law as an injury.

Attachment, See Writ of Attachment.

Averment. A positive statement of facts, in opposition
   to argument or inference.

Bankruptcy. The state or condition of one who is a bankrupt; amenability to the bankrupt laws; the condition
   of one who has committed an act of bankruptcy, and is
   liable to be proceeded against by his creditors therefor, or of one whose circumstances are such that he
   is entitled, on his voluntary application, to take
   the benefit of the bankruptcy laws. The term is used
   in a looser sense as synonymous with "insolvency,"
   the inability to pay one's debts; the stopping and
   breaking up of business because the trader is broken
   down, insolvent, ruined.

Bailiff. One to whom some authority, care, guardianship,
   or jurisdiction is delivered, committed, or intrusted.
   Court official.

Best Evidence. Primary or original evidence. The best
   and highest evidence of which the nature of the case
   is susceptible, not the highest or strongest evidence
   which thenature of the thing to be proved admits of.
   A written instrument is itself always regarded as the
   primary or best possible evidence of its existence
   and contents; a copy, or the recollection of a witness, would be secondary evidence.

Bill of Particulars. Written documentation of particulars
   in connection with and relevant to a law suit, specifying items, dates, times, and so on, submitted either
   voluntarily or on court order. An account of the items
   of a claim.

Bona fide. In good faith.

Breach of Contract.   Failure, without legal excuse, to
   perform any promise which forms the whole or part of
   a contract.

Breach of Warranty.   A violation of an agreement as to
   the condition, content, or quality of a good sale,
   not involving fraudulent misrepresentation.

Brief.   A written or printed document, prepared by counsel
   to serve as the basis for an argument upon a cause in
   an appellate court, and usually filed for the information
   of the court.

Burden of Proof.   The necessity or duty of affirmatively
   proving a fact or facts in dispute on an issue raised
   between the parties in a cause.

Cause of Action.   The fact or facts which establish or
   give rise to a right of action, the existence of which
   affords a party a right to judicial relief.   See Chapter
   III.

Certificate of Service.   A statement or assertion that a
   pleading document in litigation has been served upon
   the opposing party in the litigation.

Citation.   1.   The reading, or production of, or reference
   to, legal authorities and precedents, (such as constitutions, statutes, reported cases, and elementary
   treatises), in arguments to courts, or in legal textbooks, to establish or fortify the propositions ad-
   vanced.   2.   A writ issued out of a court of competent
   jurisdiction, commanding a person therein named to
   appear on a day named and do something therein mentioned, or show cause why he should not.

Civil Action.   An action wherein an issue is presented for
   trial formed by averments of complaint and denials in
   an answer to new matter.

Civil Court.   Courts vested with jurisdiction to handle
   civil controversies as distinguished from criminal
   cases.   Many courts do both--have concurrent jurisdiction.

Clerk.   A person employed in a public office, or as an
   officer of court, whose duty is to keep records or
   accounts.

Co-defendant. A joint defendant.

Common Law. The general and ordinary law of a community receiving its binding force from universal reception. Historically, that body of law and juristic theory which was originated, developed, and formulated in England.

Complaint. The first pleading on the part of the plaintiff in a civil action. Its purpose is to give defendant information of all material facts on which plaintiff relies to support his demand.

Compulsory Counterclaim. Claim by defendant against the plaintiff arising out of the same transaction or occurrence as stated in the complaint.

Constructive Service. Any form of service other than actual personal service; notification of an action or of some proceeding therein, given to a person affected by sending it to him in the mails or causing it to be published in a newspaper.

Contempt. A willful disregard or disobedience of a public authority.

Contract. An oral, written, or implied agreement between two or more persons; a formal covenant of undertaking; an enforceable pact.

Contributory Negligence. The act or omission amounting to want of ordinary care on the part of complaining party, which, concurring with the defendant's negligence, is the proximate cause of injury.

Controvert. To dispute; to deny; to oppose or contest; to take issue on.

Counterclaim. A claim presented by a defendant in opposition to or deduction from the claim of the plaintiff. A species of set-off or recoupment introduced by the codes of civil procedure in many of the states, of a broad and liberal character.

Court. An organ of the government, belonging to the judicial department, whose function is the application of the laws to controversies brought before it and the public administration of justice.

Court Reporter. In trial courts, a person who transcribes the testimony and proceedings in a trial or proceedings before the court.

Credibility. Worthiness of belief; that quality in a witness which renders his evidence worthy of belief. After the competence of a witness is allowed, the consideration of his credibility arises, and not before.

Criminal. 1. One who has committed a criminal offense; one who has been legally convicted of a crime; one adjudged guilty of crime. 2. That which pertains to or is connected with the law of crimes, or the administration of penal justice, or which relates to or has the character of crime.

Cross-Claim. A claim brought by a defendant against a plaintiff in the same action or against a co-defendant or both concerning matters in question in the original complaint, and its purposes are to discover facts in aid of defense, to bring in new matter in aid of defense, to obtain some affirmative relief concerning matters in issue, to obtain full relief for all parties and a complete determination of all controversies arising out of matters alleged in the original complaint, and to have affirmative relief against either plaintiff or co-defendant in the nature of an original complaint.

Cross-examination. The examination of a witness upon a trial or hearing, or upon taking a deposition, by the party opposed to the one who produced him, upon his evidence given in chief, to test its truth, to further develop it, or for other purposes.

Default. Omission, neglect or failure of any party to take steps required of him in the progress of a case. When a defendant in an action at law omits to plead within the time allowed him for that purpose, or fails to appear on the trial, he is said to make default, and the judgment entered in the case is technically called a "judgment by default."

Defendant. The person defending or denying; the party against whom relief or recovery is sought in an action or suit.

Defense. That which is offered and alleged by a party proceeded against in an action or suit, as a reason in law or fact why the plaintiff should not recover or establish what he seeks; what is put forward to diminish plaintiff's cause of action or defeat recovery.

Deposition. The testimony of a witness taken upon interrogatories, not in open court, but in pursuance of a
commission to take testimony issued by a court, or
under a general law on the subject, and reduced to
writing and duly authenticated, and intended to be
used upon the trial of an action in court.

Directed Verdict. A verdict rendered by the jury, at the
direction of the court, where the evidence is insufficient, where the overwhelming weight of the evidence
is for one party, or where the law as applied to the
facts demands such a verdict.

Discovery. The disclosure by a litigant of facts, titles,
documents, or other things which are in his exclusive
knowledge or possession, and which are necessary to
the party seeking the discovery as a part of a cause
or action pending or to be brought in another court,
or as evidence of his rights or title in such proceeding.

Duress. Unlawful constraint exercised upon a person
whereby he is forced to do some act that he otherwise
would not have done. It consists in an illegal imprisonment, or legal imprisonment used for an illegal
purpose, or threats of bodily or other harm, or other
means amounting to or tending to coerce the will of
another, and actually inducing him to do an act contrary to his free will.

Escobedo Rule. When an investigation begins to focus on
a particular suspect, and the police take the suspect
into custody to elicit incriminating testimony, the
suspect must be warned of his right to remain silent
and to consult with an attorney. If these provisions
are not met, the Escobedo Rule maintains that no
statement made by the suspect while being interrogated
may be used against him in a criminal action.
Escobedo v. Illinois, 378 U.S. 478 (1964).

Evidence. Any species of proof, or probative matter,
legally presented at the trial of an issue, by the
act of the parties and through the medium of witnesses,
records, documents, concrete objects, etc., for the
purpose of inducing belief in the minds of the court
or jury as to their contentions.

Ex Parte. On one side only; by or for one party; done
for, in behalf of, or on the application of, one party
only.

Faretta Case. U.S. Supreme Court decision which held that a state cannot "constitutionally hale a person into its criminal courts and there force a lawyer upon him, even when he insists that he wants to conduct his own defense. Faretta v. California, 422 U.S. 806 (1975).

Fourteenth Amendment (U.S. Constitution). It became a part of the organic law July 28, 1868, and its importance entitles it to special mention. It creates or at least recognizes for the first time a citizenship of the United States, as distinct from that of the states; forbids the making or enforcement by any state of any law abridging the privileges and immunities of citizens of the United States; and secures all "persons" against any state action which is either deprivation of life, liberty, or property without due process of law or denial of equal protection of the laws.

Fraud. An intentional perversion of truth for the purpose of inducing another, in reliance upon it, to part with some valuable thing belonging to him or to surrender a legal right; a false representation of a matter of fact, whether by words or by conduct, by false or misleading representations, or by concealment of that which should have been disclosed, which deceives, and is intended to deceive another so that he shall act upon it to his legal detriment.

Garnishment. See Writ of Garnishment.

Golden Rule Argument. Argument to a jury to "put yourselves in the place of" one of the parties. It is improper because the jury is by law required to be objective and fair to all parties.

Hearing. Proceeding of relative formality, generally public, with definite issues of fact or of law to be tried, in which parties proceed against each other and have a right to be heard; it is much the same as a trial and may terminate in final orders. The word is synonymous with trial, and includes the reception of evidence and arguments thereon.

Hearsay. Evidence not proceeding from the personal knowledge of the witness, but from the mere repetition of what he has heard others say. That which does not derive its value solely from the credit of the witness, but rests mainly on the veracity and competency of

other persons. The very nature of the evidence shows
its weakness, and it is admitted only in specified
cases from necessity. It is second-hand evidence, as
distinguished from original evidence; it is the repetition at second-hand of what would be original evidence
if given by the person who originally made the statement. Literally, it is what the witness says he heard
another person say.

Immaterial. Not material, essential, or necessary; not
important or pertinent; not decisive; of no substantial consequence; without weight; of no significance.

Impertinent. That which does not belong to the pleading,
interrogatory or other proceeding; out of place; superfluous; irrelevant. A term applied to matter not necessary to constitute a cause of action or ground of
defense. It constitutes surplusage.

Inference. A truth or proposition drawn from another
which is supposed or admitted to be true. A process
of reasoning by which a fact or proposition sought to
be established is deducted as a logical consequence
from the other facts, or a state of facts, already
proved or admitted.

Interrogatory. A set or series of written questions
drawn up and propounded by one party and served on
an adversary, who must serve written answers thereto
under oath.

Jurisdiction. The word is a term of large and compre-
hensive import, and embraces every kind of judicial
action. It is the authority by which courts and
judicial officers take cognizance of and decide cases;
the legal right by which judges exercise their authority. It exists when court has cognizance of class
of cases involved, proper parties are present, and
the point to be decided is within the issues.

Jury. A certain number of men or women, selected according to law, and sworn to inquire of certain matters
of fact, and declare the truth upon evidence to be
laid before them. This definition embraces and includes various subdivisions of juries.

Laches. Laches is, or is based on, delay attended by or
inducing change of condition or relation. Estoppel
by laches means a failure to do something which should
be done or to claim or enforce a right at a proper time.
A neglect to do something which one should do, or to seek
to enforce a right at a proper time.

Lack of Jurisdiction. The phrase may mean lack of power to act in a particular manner or to give certain kinds of relief. It may consist in the court's total want of power to act at all, or lack of power to act in a particular case because conditions essential to the exercise of jurisdiction have not been complied with.

Lien. A claim or charge on property for payment of some debt, obligation or duty.

Litigation. Contest in a court of justice for the purpose of enforcing a right. A judicial contest, a judicial controversy, a suit at law; a civil action.

Long Arm Statute. A statute allowing a court to obtain jurisdiction over a defendant located outside the normal jurisdiction of the court.

Miranda Rule. When a person is taken into custody, and prior to any interrogation, he must be warned that he has the right to remain silent, that any statement he makes may be used against him, that he has the right to speak to an attorney, and that if he cannot afford an attorney one will be appointed for him if he so desires. Unless these warnings are given or the rights are waived, the Miranda Rule maintains that no evidence obtained from an interrogation is allowed in court. Miranda v. Arizona, 384 U.S. 346 (1966).

Misrepresentation. Any manifestation by words or other conduct by one person to another that, under the circumstances, amounts to an assertion not in accordance with the facts. An untrue statement of fact. An incorrect or false representation. That which, if accepted, leads the mind to an apprehension of a condition other and different from that which exists. False and fraudulent misrepresentation is a representation contrary to the fact, made by a person with a knowledge of its falsehood, and being the cause of the other party's entering into the contract. Negligent misrepresentation is a false representation made by a person who has no reasonable grounds for believing it to be true, though he does not know that it is untrue, or even believes it to be true.

Mistrial. An erroneous, invalid, or nugatory trial; a trial of an action which cannot stand in law because of want of jurisdiction, or a wrong drawing of jurors, or disregard of some other fundamental requisite.

Motion. An application for an order to a court or judge; a motion addressed to the discretion of the court.

Payment. The fulfillment of a promise, or the perform- ance of an agreement; a discharge of an obligation or debt, and part payment, if accepted, is a discharge pro tanto (as far as it goes).

Perjury. The willful assertion as to a matter of fact, opinion, belief, or knowledge, made by a witness in a judicial proceeding as part of his evidence, either upon oath or in any form allowed by law to be substi- tuted for an oath, whether such evidence is given in open court, or in an affidavit, or otherwise, such assertion being material to the issue or point of inquiry and known to such witness to be false.

Permissive Counterclaim. An action by a defendant against a plaintiff arising out of a "transaction or occurrence" not the same as the subject of a claim of plaintiff against the defendant.

Plaintiff. A person who brings an action; the party who complains or sues in a personal action and is so named on the record.

Pleading. The formal allegations by the parties of their respective claims and defenses, for the judgment of the court.

Preemptory Challenge. A challenge to a prospective juror, in jury selection, disqualifying him from being empanel- ed for no stated reason. The number of preemptory challenges varies and is established by statute.

Preponderance of Evidence. Greater weight of evidence, or evidence which is more credible and convincing to the mind. That which best accords with reason and probability. The word "preponderance" means something more than "weight;" it denotes a superiority of weight, or outweighing. The words are not synonymous, but substantially different. There is generally weight" of evidence on each side in a case of contested facts. But juries cannot properly act upon the weight of evidence, in favor of one having the onus, unless it overbears, in some degree, the weight upon the other side.

Prima Facie Case. Such as will suffice until contradicted
    and overcome by other evidence. A case which has pro-
    ceeded upon sufficient proof to that stage where it will
    support finding if evidence to the contrary is disregarded.

Pro Se. For himself; in his own behalf; in person.

Rebuttal. The introduction of rebuttal evidence; the
    showing that statement of witnesses as to what occur-
    red is not true; the stage of a trial at which such
    evidence may be introduced; also the rebutting evid-
    ence itself.

Redundancy. This is the fault of introducing superfluous
    matter into a legal instrument; particularly the inser-
    tion in a pleading of matters foreign, extraneous, and
    irrelevant to that which it is intended to answer.

Release. The relinquishment, concession, or giving up
    of a right, claim, or privilege, by the person in whom
    it exists or to whom it accrues, to the person against
    whom it might have been demanded or enforced.

Reply. In its general sense, that which a plaintiff, or
    other party who has instituted a proceeding says in
    answer to the defendant's counterclaim or answer.

Res Judicata. A matter adjudged; a thing judicially
    acted upon or decided; a thing or matter settled by
    judgment.

Rule 12 Motions. The pleadings and motions authorized
    by Federal Rule 12 and those state rules patterned after
    it. See Chapter III.

Scintilla of Evidence. A spark of evidence. A metaphor-
    ical expression to describe a very insignificant or
    trifling item or particle of evidence; used in the
    statement of the common law rule that if there is any
    evidence at all in a case, even a mere scintilla,
    tending to support a material issue, the case cannot
    be taken from the jury, but must be left to their
    decision.

Second-hand Evidence. Evidence which has passed through
    one or more media before reaching the witness; hear-
    say evidence.

Service of Process. The service of writs, summonses, rules, etc., signifies the delivering to or leaving them with the party to whom or with whom they ought to be delivered or left; and, when they are so delivered, they are then said to have been served. Usually a copy only is served and the original is shown.

Statute of Frauds. This is the common designation of a very celebrated English statute (29 Car. II. C. 3) passed in 1677, and which has been adopted in a more or less modified form, in all states in this country. Its chief characteristic is the provision that no suit or action shall be maintained on certain classes of contracts or engagements unless there shall be a note or memorandum thereof in writing signed by the party to be charged or by his authorized agent. Its object was to close the door to the numerous frauds and perjuries.

Statute of Limitations. A statute imposing limits on the period during which certain rights, as the collection of debts, may be legally enforced.

Subpoena. A process to cause a witness to appear and give testimony, commanding him to lay aside all pretenses and excuses, and appear before a court or magistrate therein named at a time therein mentioned to testify for the party named under penalty therein mentioned.

Substituted Service. Service of process upon a defendant in any manner, authorized by statute, other than personal service within the jurisdiction; as by publication, by mailing a copy to his last known address, or by personal service in another state.

Summary Judgment. A judgment rendered on a motion by a party to a lawsuit, where pleadings, depositions, interrogatories, admissions, and other evidence show that there is no issue as to any material fact, and that the movant is entitled to a judgment as a matter of law. See Rule 56.

Summons. A writ, directed to the sheriff or other proper officer, requiring him to notify the person named that an action has been commenced against him in the court whence the writ issued, and that he is required to appear, on a day named, and answer the complaint in such action.

Trial. A judicial examination, in accordance with the
    law of the land, of a cause, either civil or criminal,
    of the issues between the parties, whether of law or
    fact, before a court that has jurisdiction over it.

Venue. A neighborhood; the place, or county in which an
    injury is declared to have been done, or fact declared
    to have happened. A venue which must be laid in a
    particular county.

Void. Having no legal or binding force; null. Empty or
    not containing matter; vacant; unoccupied; devoid;
    destitute.

Waiver. The intentional or voluntary relinquishment of
    a known right, or such conduct as warrants an infer-
    ence of the relinquishment of such right. The renun-
    ciation, repudiation, abandonment, or surrender of
    some claim, right, privilege, or of the opportunity
    to take advantage of some defect, irregularity, or
    wrong.

Witness. One who, being present, personally sees or per-
    ceives a thing; a beholder, spectator, or eyewitness.
    One who testifies to what he has seen, heard, or other-
    wise observed.

Writ of Attachment. A writ employed to enforce obdience
    to an order or judgment of the court. It may take
    the form of commanding the sheriff to attach the dis-
    obedient party and to have him before the court to
    answer his contempt.

Writ of Execution. A writ to put in force the judgment
    or decree of a court.

Writ of Garnishment. A warning to a person in whose
    hands the effects of another are attached, not to pay
    the money or deliver the property of the defendant in
    his hands to him, but to appear and answer the plain-
    tiff's suit. A statutory proceeding whereby a person's
    property, money, or credits in possession or under con-
    trol of, or owing by, another are applied to payment
    of the former's debt to third person by proper statu-
    tory process against debtor and garnishee.

APPENDIX

BIBLIOGRAPHY OF LAW BOOKS

American Jurisprudence, Second (Am Jur 2d)
Am Jur, Legal Forms
Am Jur, Pleading and Practice Forms
Am Jur, Proof of Facts
Am Jur, Trials
American Law Reports (ALR)
ALR 2d
ALR 3d
ALR FED
Bender, Federal Practice Manual
Bender, Federal Practice Forms
Bender, Forms of Discovery
Black's Law Dictionary, Fourth Edition
Corpus Juris Secondum (C.J.S.)
California Discovery Practice
California Pretrial and Settlement Procedures
California Procedures, Second
Federal Civil Practice, Harold A. Kooman
Federal Jury Practice and Instructions, Second, 1970
Federal Practice Digest
Federal Practice & Procedure, Barron & Holtzoff
Florida Civil Practice Before Trial, Third CLE (1975)
Interrogatories: Basic Facts, Douglas Danner 1970
Jury Instructions (Your State)
Law of Evidence, Charles T. McCormick
Law of Federal Courts, Second, 1970, Charles Allen Wright
Martindale-Hubbell Law Digest, Volume VI
New York Civil Practice, Weinstein & Korn
United States Code Annotated
United States Code Service
Words and Phrases

West Report System:

Atlantic Reports; and A 2d	CT, DE, DC, ME, MD, NH, NJ, PA, RI, VT
Northeastern Reports; and N.E. 2d	IL, IN, MA, NY, OH
Northwestern Reports; and N.W. 2d	IA, MI, MN, NE, SD, WI
Pacific Reports; and P 2d	AK, AZ, CA, CO, HI, ID, KS, MT, NV, NM, OK, OR, UT, WA, WY
Southeastern Reports; and S.E. 2d	GA, SC, NC, VA, WV
Southwestern Reports; and S.W. 2d	AR, MO, KY, TN, TX
Southern Reports; and So 2d	AL, LA, FL, MS
Supreme Court Reports	
Federal Reports	
Federal Reports, 2d	
Federal Supplement	